A Concise History
of Kentucky

D1121196

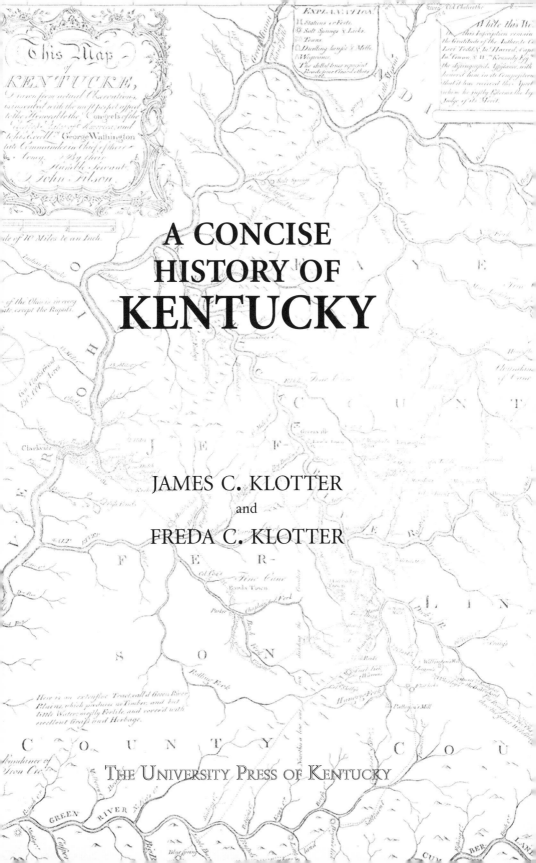

A CONCISE
HISTORY OF
KENTUCKY

JAMES C. KLOTTER

and

FREDA C. KLOTTER

THE UNIVERSITY PRESS OF KENTUCKY

Copyright © 2008 by The University Press of Kentucky

Scholarly publisher for the Commonwealth,
serving Bellarmine University, Berea College, Centre College of Kentucky,
Eastern Kentucky University, The Filson Historical Society, Georgetown
College, Kentucky Historical Society, Kentucky State University,
Morehead State University, Murray State University, Northern Kentucky
University, Transylvania University, University of Kentucky, University of
Louisville, and Western Kentucky University.
All rights reserved.

Editorial and Sales Offices: The University Press of Kentucky
663 South Limestone Street, Lexington, Kentucky 40508-4008
www.kentuckypress.com

12 11 10 09 08   5 4 3 2

Library of Congress Cataloging-in-Publication Data

Klotter, James C.
  A concise history of Kentucky / James C. Klotter and Freda C. Klotter.
     p. cm.
  Includes bibliographical references and index.
   ISBN 978-0-8131-2498-8 (alk. paper)
   ISBN 978-0-8131-9192-8 (pbk. : alk. paper)
   1. Kentucky—History. I. Klotter, Freda C., 1946–   II. Title.
  F451.K66 2008
  976.9—dc22   2007045571

This book is printed on acid-free recycled paper meeting
the requirements of the American National Standard
for Permanence in Paper for Printed Library Materials.

Manufactured in the United States of America.

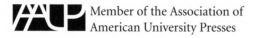 Member of the Association of
American University Presses

To our grandchildren

Contents

Preface

If nature abhors a vacuum, so too do publishers and authors. Although one of us (James C. Klotter) had coauthored the standard full history of the state and edited a high school state history textbook, and we had recently coauthored an elementary school text, none fully met the need for a concise, readable, and affordable introductory history of the Commonwealth of Kentucky and its people. To remedy that situation, this book emerged. In essence, it is a revision of a 2006 work entitled *Faces of Kentucky*. In this leaner (though not meaner) version, some features have been omitted, and some material has been added or updated to bring the freshest scholarship to the subject. Most of all, this book provides a good, solid, readable introduction to the state—past, present, and future. Here, readers can find out about the Native American frontier, early leaders such as Daniel Boone, the divisive Civil War era, the bloody feud period, the important twentieth century, and much more. Within these pages, sidebars feature the stories of the people who made the history, and materials from the time are highlighted so readers themselves can examine these sources and be historians, operating as detectives. These chapters also detail the state's government, geography, education, and economy, as well as its rich literary and cultural traditions.

This work tells the story of all Kentuckians, young and old, rich and poor, black and white, past and present, in a way that has meaning for today's readers. So, for those new to the state or just new to its history, this book was written for you. It is our hope that it entertains and educates and that reading this book will make you want to explore Kentucky's rich past even more. It is a journey worth taking.

(Map by Dick Gilbreath)

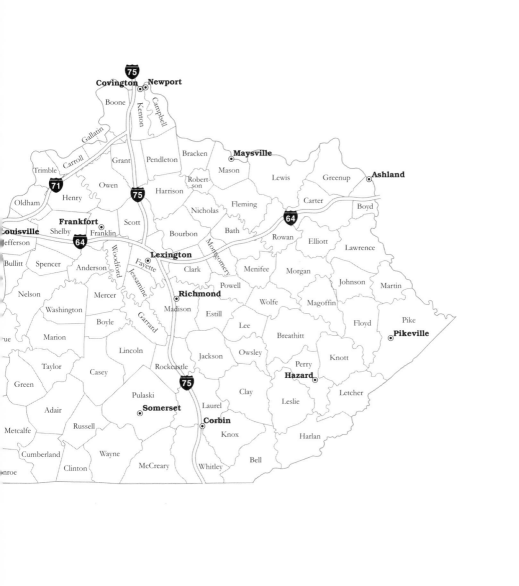

CHAPTER ONE

Frontiers—Then and Now

One meaning of the word *frontier* is a border between places. But those borders can be very different at different times.

Astronaut Dr. Story Musgrave of Kentucky first went into space in 1983. Though he was born outside the state, he learned to fly in Lexington and considered Kentucky his home. He flew on the space shuttle a total of six times, during which he helped repair a space telescope and even walked in space. When he retired, no other person had taken more space flights.

Musgrave was not the only astronaut from Kentucky. Born in Russellville, Terry Wilcutt went to high school in Louisville and got a college degree in Bowling Green. He taught math in high school for a time, then became a space shuttle pilot and participated in four flights. On one, he linked up with the space station.

Both Musgrave and Wilcutt traveled thousands of miles in just a few

Astronaut Terry Wilcutt. (Courtesy of the Kentucky Library, Western Kentucky University)

days. Both saw things that few others had seen. Both experienced a sense of wonder as they left their world for the unknowns of space. But when they faced that unknown future and the frontier of space, they were simply doing what humans have done for thousands of years.

How did the first human who stepped on the soil of what is now Kentucky feel? Exactly when that event happened, and who that person was, are unknown. But that first person (one of a group called Indians or Native Americans) started the process of people living in Kentucky—and it still goes on. The first Kentuckian could travel only a few miles on foot each day. Yet as that person looked out over the untouched land, he or she likely felt much the same way those astronauts felt many thousands of years later. That person saw a new place that no one else had ever seen. That man or woman faced a new frontier. That person looked to a fresh future.

Many, many centuries later, people from Europe arrived at what, to them, was the New World, and they called it America. Think of how it would be today if astronauts in a space shuttle suddenly came upon a new, previously unknown planet and found that humans were already living on it. Such feelings of discovery and awe the Europeans experienced in America. They found humans they did not know even existed. The Indians, of course, had the same reaction, for these people from across the ocean were new to them too.

European explorers soon made their way to Kentucky and found a land that filled them with excitement. Like the Indians before them, they wanted to live there. They also sought a new life on this new frontier. Although living thousands of years apart, the first Indians, the first European explorers, and even the present-day astronauts from Kentucky all shared the same human feelings about the places they saw.

Today, if people want to travel to places that no one has seen before, they may have to go into space, as astronauts Musgrave and Wilcutt did. But many frontiers still exist on earth, and the spirit of those earlier people remains alive today. After all, change happens all the time. Our future may involve another meaning of the word *frontier*. It can also mean discovering new learning and the outer boundaries of knowledge. Our future frontiers may be frontiers of the mind. People may make discoveries in science or medicine, invent new ways of doing things, write books that cause people to think in different ways, or so much more. New frontiers still await present-day explorers.

The Past

People who study the past are explorers too. Similar to those who came to Kentucky many years ago, historians want to discover new things. Like detectives trying to solve the mysteries of history, they seek to uncover the hidden past.

But why? Why is history important? First of all, knowing what other people did means that current generations do not have to relearn everything. They do not have to repeat earlier mistakes and can follow the example of what worked for others. In the end, the historical record remains the only guide to how humans acted.

If people got up each morning and did not know where to go or what to eat, they would have to learn those things over and over again. They would not get much done and would make many mistakes before discovering what they needed to know. If the people living in a state or a nation do not know their history, they have to relearn all of life's lessons. That is why history is important.

History is about real people and real events. Sometimes individuals make mistakes; sometimes they act heroically and courageously in matters big and small. Those actions and those lives can be models for today. History is not just about the past; it is also about the future.

Writing about the Past

Everyone can be a historian. If you wanted to write a history of your grandparents, for example, you might first talk to them and let them tell the story of their lives—an oral history. Then you could ask other people what they know about your grandparents. You might go through family photographs or even old letters that had been saved. Reading historical city and county newspapers might reveal stories about your grandparents' past. School yearbooks could provide additional information about them. Any land or houses they bought would be listed in records in the courthouse. Finally, everything you found out could be written down as their history, their record of life on this earth. In doing those things, you would be acting as a historian, solving mysteries and explaining your grandparents' lives to others. And in the end, you would likely learn things you did not know before—about your grandparents and about yourself.

But what happens when no letters, newspapers, or other written sources are available? How can people re-create the elusive past in that case? In fact, that is the situation for most of the years that humans have lived in Kentucky. Trying to tell the story of those times becomes much more difficult. Without written records and people to interview, how can we find out about the people of the past?

Archaeologists try to find answers by studying ancient people and looking at what they left behind—stone tools, bits of pottery, pieces of clothing, burial places, skeletons, and even trash pits. If someone looked at a modern family's trash, what could they find out about them? By examining the trash of the past, archaeologists can discover what people ate, based on the animal bones or shells they threw away. They could uncover bits of broken jars and be able to determine how the people stored food and other things. They might find old pieces of arrows and understand how the ancient people made weapons. Such records can suggest how people lived thousands of years ago. What, then, do we know about the first people in Kentucky?

Native Americans in Kentucky

Native Americans (or American Indians) are not really native to America. They, too, came as immigrants. Thousands of years ago, when the land and oceans had different configurations, people from Asia could walk across a land bridge to Alaska. From there they slowly spread over America. It is possible that some also came by small boats across the Pacific Ocean. Native Americans traveled to America, then, just as other people did much later.

These new people found themselves in a new land filled with animals that they could hunt—and animals that could hunt them, too. Eventually, one Indian—or perhaps a whole family—came to what we now call Kentucky, and the first humans walked this land. That event probably happened at least 12,000 years ago. If one generation covers 20 years, then 600 generations of American Indians lived and died here before the first European explorers even arrived in America. In contrast, only a dozen or so generations have lived in Kentucky since written histories have existed. To put it another way, if every inch on a six-inch line stands for 2,000 years of history, then Europeans have been in Kentucky only one-eighth of an inch on that scale—not very long.

Change takes place over time, and archaeologists have divided those 12,000 years into four different periods, each with its own characteristics.

Paleo-Indians, 10,000 to 8000 B.C.

Paleo-Indians came to Kentucky some 12,000 years ago, in 10,000 B.C. or earlier. At that time, ice covered most of the northern part of the United States, and Kentucky had a much colder climate than it does today. Its trees resembled those in the far north today, and large lakes covered parts of the land.

Little is known about the Native Americans who walked the land then. Now-extinct animals, including huge mammoths and mastodons, roamed nearby. The Indians hunted some for food, using sharpened stone points on spears. They stayed in small camps of a few dozen people but built no houses; they used rock shelters or anything else they could find in nature. Overall, they lived hard, simple, short lives. Probably no more than 5,000 people called Kentucky home during this period.

Native Americans hunted the mammoths that roamed Kentucky, using the skin for protection from the cold and the meat for food. (Kentucky Heritage Council poster titled "Kentucky before Boone")

Although their lives differed greatly from ours, they had the same human feelings. They saw people being born and others dying. They loved and hated; they understood pleasure and pain. They laughed and cried, and they knew happiness and sorrow. They were not all alike; individual differences existed, just as today. Some had different ideas or spoke different languages. Sometimes they lived at peace with one another; at other times they fought. Not much is known about them, but they did start the process of humans living in Kentucky.

Archaic Period, 8000 to 1000 B.C.

The Archaic period, which lasted about 7,000 years, represents the longest period of Native American life in Kentucky. During that time, the land changed as the ice age ended. Inland seas disappeared, modern rivers flowed, the population increased, and people moved less. For food they killed deer, elk, beavers, birds, and turtles. They also gathered nuts and ate river mussels.

The Archaic people invented new weapons for hunting. The atlatl allowed them to throw their spears a greater distance. They made stone axes as well and used them to build dugout canoes.

Near the end of the Archaic period, a small shift took place, but it was one that would mark a major change over the years. When the American Indians in Kentucky began to grow squash—both for food and as containers—that marked the beginning of farming and a new way of life.

Woodland Period, 1000 B.C. to A.D. 1000

For 2,000 years, change took place gradually. People still mostly hunted for food and added only sunflowers and a few other plants to what they grew. But two major inventions did occur—pottery and a new weapon.

Woodland Indians in the eastern and central parts of Kentucky began making pottery around 1000 B.C. Having bowls and pots allowed them to cook directly over a fire. In that simple society, however, it took another 500 years for pottery making to reach parts of western Kentucky. Later, around A.D. 800, a new weapon arrived: the bow and arrow. Use of the bow and arrow spread rapidly, and Native Americans were soon utilizing it for both fighting and hunting.

During this time, the Indians' lifestyle grew increasingly complex.

Kentucky Lives: An Indian's Story

His name, if he had one, is lost to history. But more than 2,400 years ago, a Native American man entered Mammoth Cave to dig minerals, unaware that he was working in one of the largest cave systems in the world.

The man got up in the morning, put on a skimpy piece of clothing, and left camp for the cave. He was about fifty-four years old and stood five feet, three inches tall. Perhaps he saw his mate making barrel-shaped pots as he was leaving. Perhaps others who were tending sunflowers in the fields watched him go. That is not known. What is known is that he lit some reeds to use as torches and went three miles into the darkness of Mammoth Cave. He was high on a ledge, digging out minerals and placing them in a pouch, when a rock fell and crushed him. The cool air in the cave preserved his body for centuries. About seventy years ago, some people found his mummified remains. He is a reminder of the present's link to those who lived and died in the past.

They used axes to cut trees and clear land, which changed their environment. Objects found in burial mounds show that they also had a strong belief in life after death. But the biggest change came at the end of the Woodland period, when Native Americans began to grow maize (corn). Corn, potatoes, tobacco, and tomatoes—all American crops unknown to Europeans—led to the creation of a new farming lifestyle in the next era.

Late Prehistoric Period, A.D. 1000 to 1750

Corn-based farming produced more food, which caused a rapid increase in the number of Indians. They built larger villages and formed towns ruled by powerful chiefs. Trade expanded all the way to the Great Lakes. But such growth meant that different groups had more contact with one another, and violence increased.

Differences between the Native Americans within Kentucky became greater as well. In the west, the *Mississippian culture* consisted of large, walled villages of more than 1,000 people. Tall, flat-topped earthen pyramid platforms and a central, open plaza for sports and other events dominated these villages. Around the plaza, people built houses with pole frames, sun-baked mud walls, and grass roofs. Colorful pottery

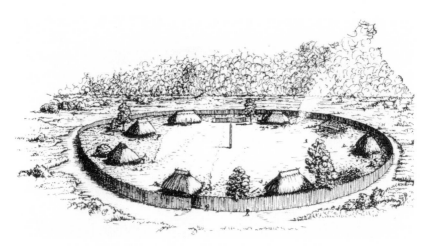

Before the Europeans came to Kentucky, Native Americans lived in fort-type communities similar to those the settlers later built. (Copyright Kentucky Heritage Council; design and artwork by Jimmy A. Railey)

and rich decorations displayed the skills of those who lived there. In contrast, in the east, a simpler society existed. Indians of the *Fort Ancient culture* used wooden walls for protection against others, but they had smaller villages and no central platform mounds. Generally, they had simpler pottery and a less sophisticated lifestyle. But whether in the eastern or western part of the state, Native American life was about to face its greatest challenge.

The Great Dying

In 1492, Christopher Columbus came to what Europeans later called the New World. At that time, thousands of Indians lived in Kentucky. Two hundred years later, however, English explorers found few tribes still living in Kentucky. By the 1750s, only two Native American towns seemed to be left, outside of far western Kentucky. One was Lower Shawneetown on the Ohio River in Greenup County. In 1751, it had some 1,200 people, but floods caused its residents to leave soon thereafter. The other town, Eskippakithiki, was in central Kentucky. Indians also abandoned this place, and it later burned. When the first wave of European settlers came to Kentucky a few years later, they found no Native Americans living there. Why?

This is a historical mystery waiting to be solved. Kentucky was a place of rich farmland with plenty of animals. It was a locale where American Indians had lived in large numbers for thousands of years. Why were the Indians gone by the 1760s?

The first part of the answer concerns the beginning of Kentucky's historical period. Written records show that various European explorers—from Spain, France, and England—first came in small numbers to Kentucky. They brought with them various items that they traded for furs. But unknowingly, these explorers also carried something else—disease.

One person wrote that the Europeans won Kentucky from the Indians not by guns but simply by being there. He meant that the diseases the Europeans brought with them killed many more Native Americans than any weapons or wars. Long before settlers arrived, invisible pioneers in the form of germs swept across Kentucky. Indians had never been exposed to these diseases, and their bodies had no means to resist them. The "Great Dying" resulted. Across America and across Kentucky, millions perished. Some say that diseases killed half of all Native Americans; others think that as many as four out of every five died.

Like an invisible wave, disease spread. It decimated populations and caused others to flee from the unknown cause of so much death. Kentucky became almost vacant for a time. Those who did not die had been weakened in many ways. Many tribes lost their leaders, and the death of those who passed down the stories from generation to generation left the tribes without a history. Native peoples now had fewer people to resist the new European forces. Land went unused because no one remained to farm it. When settlers finally came to Kentucky, the Indians they encountered were very different from those of a century before. Native Americans still claimed Kentucky as a hunting land, and conflict with the settlers ensued. But the earlier effect of disease on the Indians made it an uneven fight from the start.

The Name "Kentucky"

Native Americans left their mark on Kentucky in many ways. Perhaps the clearest example involves the name of the state itself. The exact origins remain uncertain. One version indicates that *Kentucky* came from an Indian word *Kenta-ke,* meaning "a place of fields" or "a level place" or "meadowland." Another source says that it came from another tribe's name for the area—*Ken-tah-teh,* meaning "tomorrow" or "land of tomorrow."

Whatever the exact meaning, European explorers took what they heard and changed it to fit their language. As early as the 1750s, people called the land Kentucky. Later, some would erroneously say that the name meant "dark and bloody ground." An Indian chief had once predicted that when settlers went there, they would find a dark cloud hanging over the place, and attempts to settle it would end in bloodshed. The peaceful "meadowland" or "land of tomorrow" would indeed soon be known as a place of conflict.

CHAPTER TWO

Starting a State

In its early days, Kentucky became a middle ground. It served as a crossroads where different groups met. Native Americans hunted the land. From the north and west, small groups of French explorers came to the region. A few Spanish arrived from the South. From the east, Virginians and other English colonists, and the African Americans they brought with them, entered Kentucky. It was a multicultural society from the start.

When these groups made peaceful contact, they could see how each had changed the others' lives. By then, the Indian villages, with their cabins and walls, looked much like the English stockades. Indians and Europeans wore similar clothes on the frontier. Most adopted the Native American moccasin, and they combined European clothing with Indian items. Quickly the native people started replacing the bow and arrow with the rifle.

Clear divisions did not exist among the different groups of people. Just as the English fought the French, different Indian tribes fought each other. Sometimes one tribe would support the French, while another would side with the English. As the Europeans divided, so did the Native Americans.

When the groups came together, they did so to barter and trade. Europeans would bring cheap jewelry, metal goods, weapons, mirrors, and strong drink, among other things. The Indians would exchange deerskins, beaver furs, and other items. They would talk back and forth until both sides agreed on a trade.

Even though the two worlds—European and Indian—often seemed similar, they also differed. Those differences sometimes made compromise difficult, and people died as a result.

Europeans in Kentucky most often made contact with the Shawnee tribe of Indians, who lived in Ohio and hunted and traded in Kentucky. They built houses about twenty feet long, covered in tree bark. Shawnee men hunted, while the women farmed. The Shawnee concept that no one owned the land caused part of the conflict with the European settlers.

Kentucky Voices

Daniel Trabue came to Kentucky in 1785, when he was twenty-five years old. Near the end of his life, while living in Columbia in Adair County, he wrote down his memories of those early days. Here he relates a talk he had with an Indian chief, one that shows how the two groups held different views of land.

This chief said to me . . . "What do you want to take Indian land from them for?"

I told him that we alwaise bought their land and paid them for it.

He said he beleaved that the Great Spirrett made all the people. . . . He made all the land and it was the Great Sperritt's land. And it was rong for Indian or white man to say it was his land. This was a lie.

"Now," said he, "if Indian make house, it is Indean's house. If he make corn field, it is his, but the land is the Great Spirrett's. But," said he, "the white man he marke of[f] the land in the woods and say it is his land." Said he: "This is a lie. It is not his land. It is the Great Sperritt's land."

The Shawnee raised their children to be tough. They tied their babies to cradle boards to make sure that they would grow straight and strong. The boards also left flat spots on the backs of the babies' heads. Shawnee mothers bathed their children in cold water every day, even in winter, to harden them. Overall, Shawnee women had much more freedom than European women, and as a result, European women who were captured by the Shawnee sometimes did not want to return to their own people. Because so many members of the tribe had died of disease, the Indians often adopted these white captives into their tribes and treated them as part of the family. The settlers seldom dealt with captured Indians in the same way.

But the major conflicts came over animals and land. Simon Girty, a white man who had switched sides and become a leader of the Indians, spoke to a group of tribes and told them why they should fight:

The Indians from all the tribes, have had a right from time imme-morial, to hunt and kill unmolested these wild animals. . . .

Kentucky Lives: Mary Ingles

Mary Draper Ingles may have been the first European woman in Kentucky, although she certainly did not want to have that privilege.

In 1755, Mary and her husband lived in a house in scenic frontier Virginia. No English lived in Kentucky, and none would for another twenty years. At that time, Mary was twenty-three years old and had been married for six years. She had two sons—Thomas, age four, and George, age two—and was expecting a third child. Then, on July 8, her happy life changed when Indians raided her settlement. They killed several people and captured Mary Ingles and her sons. Three days after being taken captive, she gave birth to a daughter. The next day she got back on a horse with her baby and continued to ride. The Native Americans took her to their camp in Ohio and seized her sons.

Three months later, the Indians and Mary Ingles went to Big Bone Lick, in what is now Boone County in northern Kentucky, to get salt. The Indians forced her to leave her baby daughter behind. Mary decided that this might be her only chance to escape, so she fled. She trudged through the wilderness for forty days. Thorn bushes tore off most of her clothes. Her feet grew swollen and bloody. She had little food and became almost too weak to stand. Then, at last, Mary reached a cabin near her home. It had been nearly half a year since her capture. She was reunited with her husband, and they moved away from the frontier. Just days after they left, Indians attacked the house where they had been staying and killed or captured everyone there. Mary had narrowly escaped becoming a prisoner again.

Mary and her husband had four more children. Thirteen years after her capture, Mary learned that her son Thomas, now seventeen years old, had been located. He lived with a Native American family and could no longer speak English. After being with the Indians for so long, he was reluctant to leave, and when he finally did return to his mother, he never fully accepted his new life. Mary never saw her daughter or her son George again. Deeply saddened, she was forever changed by her experience. She died at age eighty-three, with the dubious distinction of being the first non-Indian woman in Kentucky.

Brothers, the Long Knives [the people from Virginia] have overrun your country and usurped your hunting grounds—they have . . . killed . . . the deer and the buffaloe, the bear and the raccoon. . . .

> Unless you rise . . . and exterminate their whole race, you may bid adieu to the hunting grounds of your fathers.

Because the English showed little desire to do anything other than take and occupy the land, conflict followed.

The First West

The various Europeans in North America—French, Spanish, and English—had all been in the land called Kentucky at one time or another. The English, however, would be the ones to settle the land, although a century passed between the first English venture into Kentucky and the first settlement there.

Part of the reason for the delay had to do with geography. The Appalachian Mountains form a barrier between Kentucky and the area farther east. Early explorers called these the "Endless Mountains" because it took so long to cross them. Most people went around the Appalachian Mountains and came into Kentucky through a break called the Cumberland Gap. Another way to reach Kentucky was to go down the Ohio River on a boat. Most people got off the boat at Maysville or Louisville or went up the Kentucky River to central Kentucky.

Either trip brought the English explorers into contact with the Native Americans who initially lived in Kentucky and later just hunted here. Those Indians represented the second reason it took so long for the English to settle in Kentucky. Conflict between the two groups made Kentucky a dangerous place.

A third reason for the delay in settlement was that, at first, the English had plenty of land where they lived in the East. But over the years, increasing numbers of people came to America from Europe, and all of them wanted farmland on which to raise crops. As eastern land became scarce, some looked to Kentucky as a place where they could find land and fulfill their dreams.

Kentucky would become the first area to be settled outside of the original thirteen colonies. It had taken people more than a century to go just a few hundred miles inland from the ocean. Now, in just one more century, explorers and settlers would cover the whole continent. America's first step westward took place in Kentucky and set the stage for all later expansion. Thus, Kentucky became the first West.

The First Explorers

Englishmen explored or hunted in Kentucky a century before any Europeans settled in the area. Most of them left no record of their visits, but a few carved their names in the bark of trees to show that they had been here.

By the 1750s, some explorers began to write down what they saw on their trips, with Christopher Gist and Thomas Walker being among the first to do so. Traders had already been to Kentucky to barter for furs. Then a group called the Long Hunters came to Kentucky to procure their own furs. Finally, people came just to look over the land so that later settlers would know where to find the best places.

Kentucky Voices

Two of the earliest written records of English explorers in Kentucky come from Thomas Walker and Christopher Gist. Both men were sent to find good land for others to claim as their own. Both kept journals of their trips.

Dr. Thomas Walker tells of finding the Cumberland Gap and going into eastern Kentucky in 1750, where he and those with him built perhaps the first European cabin in Kentucky:

April 13th. We went . . . six miles to Cave [Cumberland] Gap, the land being levil. . . . On the South side is a plain Indian Road. On top of the Ridge are Laurel Trees marked with crosses, others blazed and several figures on them.

23rd. We all crossed the [Cumberland] River . . . leaving the others to provide and salt some Bear, build an house, and plant some Peach Stones and Corn.

Walker never got to the Bluegrass region, and he turned to cross back into Virginia.

Christopher Gist came down the Ohio River instead, traveling through northern and central Kentucky before returning to Virginia. He wrote in 1751:

Monday [March] 18—We turned from Salt Lick Creek to a Ridge of Mountains that made toward the Cuttaway River [Kentucky River], & from the Top of the Mountain We saw a fine level Country as far as our eyes coud behold. ▶

Later, he moved into the mountains of Kentucky before leaving the state. He wrote:

Sunday [March] *24—We had but poor Food for our Horses & both We and They were very much wearied.*
   Monday [March] *25—We killed a Buck Elk and took out his Tongue to carry with Us.*

All these groups came on horseback or by boat. Many had slaves with them, so black and white alike came to Kentucky beginning in the early days. The explorers and hunters wore shirts made of linen or hemp and covered their heads with broad-brimmed hats. Almost no one—not even Daniel Boone—wore coonskin caps.

They could carry only a few things with them to the frontier. In rolled

Kentucky Lives: Monk Estill

Many people came to Kentucky for freedom: freedom of religion, freedom of political beliefs, or freedom from poverty. The ability to choose freedom did not always extend to black Americans, however, because some of the settlers brought slaves with them.

One of those enslaved people was named Monk. He stood about five feet, five inches tall and weighed 200 pounds. In March 1782, some Indians attacked a place called Estill's Station, just south of Richmond, Kentucky. They captured Monk, but he tricked the Indians into leaving, convincing them that Estill's Station was better defended than it actually was. Monk's owner, James Estill, and about twenty-five men followed the Indians, and the two forces met near Little Mountain, named for the Indian mounds there (present-day Mount Sterling). In the fierce fight that followed, Monk yelled out his captors' location, and in the ensuing confusion, Monk escaped. However, the Native Americans killed James Estill and others, and the settlers had to retreat. The battle became known as Estill's Defeat. Monk carried one of the wounded men back to the fort, more than twenty-five miles away. His new master freed him for his bravery.

Monk Estill was already the father of the first African American child born at Boonesborough. Now, as a free man, he had many more children and in his long life supported his family by making gunpowder. But the freedom he won on the frontier went to very few other slaves.

up blankets tied behind them on their horses, they might have some soap, a razor, some tobacco, and a bullet mold so that they could melt spent bullets and reuse them. The explorers might also carry a little food in their packs—coffee, flour, and sugar. Most of the time, they killed what they needed to eat—bears, buffalo, deer, turkeys, even swans.

After they made their way through the Cumberland Gap or down the Ohio River, they went into the interior of Kentucky. Once more the environment—the geography—shaped their actions. There, they found the level land they sought to farm and streams or rivers to provide water for themselves, their animals, and the land itself. They told others about this special land, and the word *Kentucky* began to have a magical appeal.

What They Found

Early explorers called Kentucky "a new found Paradise," a heaven on earth, "the Garden of the West." Animals seemed to be everywhere. Huge buffalo herds numbering a thousand or more roamed the land. One woman recalled a herd she saw near Lexington: "The woods roared with their tramping, almost as bad as thunder." Daniel Boone said, "They were more frequent than I have seen cattle in the settlements."

Buffalo created the first roads in Kentucky. As the large animals moved

---

Kentucky Voices

Laurence Butler came down the Ohio River to Kentucky in 1784 and wrote to his friends, describing what he saw:

This river affords a vast quantity of fresh water fish; they have a kind that is called cat, which weighs upward of 100 weight. . . . I remained at the Fall [Louisville] a few days and then traveled up the country to examine the land, which exceeded anything I ever saw.

It is a fine country for horses. There is the greatest plenty of buffaloes, which serve for beef; and bears, which answer the same as bacon; and, as to wild turkeys, there is no end to them.

Thirteen years later, Gilbert Imlay published a book in which he told of the rich land: "Everything here assumes a dignity and splendour I have never seen in any other part of the world. Everything here gives delight."

Daniel Trabue, however, recalled the hard winter of 1779–1780: *The* ▶

> *turkeys was almost all dead. The buffaloes had gone poore. People's cattle mostly Dead. No corn. The people was in great Distress. Many in the wilderness frostbit. Some Dead. . . . A number of people would be Taken sick and did actuly die from the want of solid food.*
>
> Another person wrote a letter from Harrodsburg and said of that same winter: *The world never new human nature so defased as the unhappy settlers that set out late for this place, many of them still remaining in the wilderness, having lost every horse & cow they were possessed of & hole families have perished on the rode, while others escaping with the loss of their hands & feet & all the skin and flesh taken off their face by the excessive cold.*

from one place to another, seeking the salt they needed, they took the easiest routes, going around mountains instead of over them and crossing rivers at the lowest water level. They cleared the area around them by eating plants as they walked. Year after year, century after century, they had traveled the same routes, creating large trails, or traces. Explorers told of one of these traces near Frankfort: "The buffalo trace at this point is 100 feet wide and in some places, the hoofs of buffalo have worn down the ground several feet." Another trace in Shelby County measured forty feet wide and four feet deep. All across Kentucky, those buffalo trails gave early explorers paths to follow. Many modern-day highways were built along buffalo traces started thousands of years ago.

The buffalo was only one of many animals in Kentucky, and the area became known as a hunting ground without rival. One person estimated that a ten-mile square of forest would contain 1 to 3 wolves, 2 or 3 panthers, 2 elk, 5 bears, 30 foxes, 200 turkeys, 400 deer and buffalo, and 10,000 squirrels. Later, settlers would go on all-day squirrel hunts to rid the land of what they considered pests that destroyed their crops. They killed 7,941 squirrels during one hunt; in another squirrel hunt in Madison County, 8,857 died. Many fur-bearing animals, such as beavers, otters, and minks, lived in or near streams. In the forests, various animals chewed off small branches and thinned out the woods as they tramped through them, providing early hunters with easy-to-follow trails in a park-like setting.

Birds seemed to be everywhere as well. Ravens, woodpeckers, and parakeets filled the air, as did passenger pigeons. One man stood and watched for four hours while a mile-wide flock of pigeons flew over. He

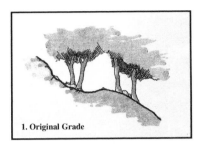

1. Original Grade

2. Bison/Indian Path

3. Indian/Explorer/Long Hunter Path

4. Wagon Trail

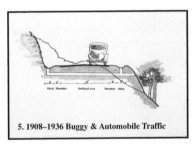

5. 1908–1936 Buggy & Automobile Traffic

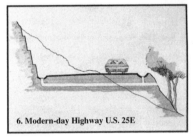

6. Modern-day Highway U.S. 25E

Buffalo trails served as the first roads. Later, people and their vehicles made those trails larger. (Courtesy of the Bell County Historical Society; from David M. Burns, *Gateway: Dr. Thomas Walker and the Opening of Kentucky* [2000])

calculated that more than *2 billion* birds had passed by. Settlers killed those birds in huge numbers.

Besides the plentiful animals, the best thing Kentucky had to offer settlers was land. One leader wrote, "A richer and more beautiful country than this, I believe has never been seen in America yet." He added that if a person saw the place once, "he never will rest until he gets in it to live." Later, a man who had traveled widely wrote to his friends that in Kentucky he had found "the richest land in the world." Another praised the tall grass, giant trees, and rich soil. In fact, those who first farmed the land claimed that it grew twice as much as the old, worn-out soil back beyond the mountains. In one writer's opinion, "this country is more temperate and healthy than the other settled parts of America." Such words made Kentucky seem like a very appealing place. But the image and the reality did not always coincide.

Coming to Kentucky

Having heard about the richness of this new place called Kentucky, many settlers made it their destination. But migrants faced hard choices. If they came into Kentucky through the Cumberland Gap, they had to walk the several hundred miles or perhaps, if they were lucky, take a horse or two. As a result, they could bring few things with them. For most people, the trip took at least four long, tiring weeks. They also faced the danger of being killed in Indian attacks or accidents.

Settlers who set out for Kentucky from Pittsburgh, going down the Ohio River, could take a few more belongings in their boats. Mary Dewees, for example, made the trip in a forty-foot-long craft. River travel was also faster, allowing settlers to reach Kentucky in just one or two weeks. But river travel cost more, so poorer people could not afford it. It also proved more dangerous, because the river took people closer to the Indian towns north of the river.

Early copper engraving of the Cumberland Gap. (Engraving by H. Fenn; published by D. Appleton & Co., New York, 1872)

Going to Kentucky meant that individuals would likely never again see their families and friends who stayed behind. It meant leaving a safe home for an unsafe one and leaving an easy life for a harder one—at least for a time. It meant going from the known and familiar to the unknown and unfamiliar of Kentucky. But the promise of good land and a fresh start in a new place drove many settlers to take the risk. They wanted better lives for themselves and for their children and thus made the hard choice: they started out for Kentucky. Some found what they sought; others did not. Many achieved success; others failed. Certain people became leaders and found fame; others found only hardship or even death.

Settling a State

Not all parts of Kentucky were settled at the same time. The first large groups of settlers came in the 1770s to central Kentucky, around Lexington, Frankfort, and Louisville. Over the next decade, others settled the northern, south-central, and western regions. By the 1790s, people began to live in eastern Kentucky. Few people lived in the westernmost parts of Kentucky before 1810 to 1820. Geography was responsible for some of that difference, with level areas being settled first. The Indian threat also made a big difference. No matter when people came to the frontiers in Kentucky, however, they all began to build homes out of the wilderness. Soon, they would create a new state.

The first Kentucky frontier, and the first part of the region to be settled, was the central part of the Bluegrass. It would also be the scene of the bloodiest battles with Native Americans who did not want to give up the land. In the first fifteen years of the English settlement of Kentucky, about 73,000 people arrived, and 1,500 or more died in conflicts with the Indians. In just one year in the area around Louisville, 131 settlers were killed or captured by the Indians—or one-eighth of the population. One person wrote, "We can hardly pass a spot, which does not remind us of the murder of a father, a brother, or a deceased friend." Native Americans probably said the same thing. On the frontier, every man and woman had to act almost like a soldier. Even children helped, for youth ended early on the frontier.

In these dangerous times, strong leaders came forward. Their efforts helped settle Kentucky and then make it safer for those who lived there.

Kentucky Voices

Daniel Drake came to Mayslick, Kentucky, in 1788, when he was only three years old. He and Kentucky grew up together. Later he became a doctor and taught in Lexington, Louisville, and Cincinnati. Near the end of his life, he wrote down his memories of those early days. Here he tells about one of his duties as a young boy in a log cabin:

The children were told at night, "lie still and go to sleep, or the Shawnees will catch you." On the morning the first duty was to ascend a ladder . . . to the loft and look through the cracks for Indians lest they might have planted themselves near the door, to rush in when the heavy crossbar should be removed. . . . But no attack was ever made.

Brave and often fearless, the earliest leaders included James Harrod, Daniel Boone, Benjamin Logan, Simon Kenton, George Rogers Clark, and many more.

The tall, bearded James Harrod established the first permanent English settlement in Kentucky. On June 16, 1774, he led a small group of men down the Ohio River and then up the Kentucky River to what they called Harrodstown, or Fort Harrod (present-day Harrodsburg). The threat of Indians drove the settlers away at first, but they came back the next year and stayed. Harrod, born in Pennsylvania, had little formal schooling, but he learned several Native American languages, as well as French, while hunting in the area north of the Ohio River. His brother and several friends would die at the hands of Indians, but Harrod never hated the Indians. In fact, many of the English leaders simply wanted to live in peace and hunt and farm, as did the Indians. That the two groups could not resolve their conflicts and live together peacefully would produce sad results.

To protect themselves, settlers at Harrodsburg and other places built forts or stations. Inside the forts sat log cabins about 20 feet square, with floors of either wood planks (whose splinters might hurt bare feet) or just dirt. The chimneys were made of stone, sticks, straw, and mud. Few cabins had windows; for those that had window spaces, they were either left open or covered with greased paper. None had glass, for it broke too easily and could not be brought to the frontier. Fort Harrod was 264 feet

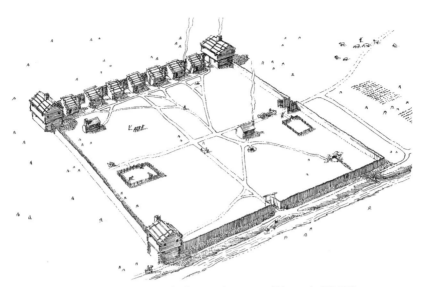

Fort Harrod. (Clay Lancaster, *Antebellum Architecture of Kentucky* [1991])

square, with 10-foot walls made of oak tree trunks placed side by side in the ground. At each corner of the fort, a larger blockhouse provided more protection if an attack came.

People did not like to live in the forts and moved away as soon as it was safe to do so. They had come to farm, not to fight. Besides that, the forts were dirty. The water supply near Fort Harrod contained all kinds of refuse and pollution from the fort, making it nearly unfit to drink. Also, the smell of horses and other animals, along with their waste, filled the air. In the summer, dust and bugs got into the cabins. In the winter, mud covered the ground outside, and smoke stung the residents' eyes inside. Forts were also crowded, and disease spread rapidly. Two years after its construction, Fort Harrod had 198 people—10 percent were slaves, 35 percent were white children, and 12 percent were white women. They all worked to protect the fort if an attack came. And they all were anxious to move outside the fort's prison-like walls as soon as they could.

Another early settlement in Kentucky was called St. Asaph's and then Logan's Fort (present-day Stanford). Although he did not start the settlement, Benjamin Logan soon guided it. A tall man with long, curly black hair, he said what he thought, which made some people mad. His skills as a leader kept the settlers alive in bad times, however.

Daniel Boone

The other major settlement in early Kentucky—and the second one to be built—was Fort Boonesborough. It was started by Daniel Boone, the most famous of the early pioneers. But why is he so famous, while others who made similar contributions are not? For one thing, a man named John Filson told Boone's story in the first book written about Kentucky—*The Discovery, Settlement, and Present State of Kentucke* (1784). It made Boone famous all over the world, while other leaders such as Harrod, Kenton, and Logan received little attention. Later, people would use Filson's book to write their own accounts of Boone's life, and much later, motion pictures and a television series added to his fame. According to Filson, Daniel Boone was born into a Quaker family in Pennsylvania. Although the Quakers believed that people should live in peace, Boone would end up playing a big part in a very violent time in history. He never went to school, but his son said that Boone could "read, spell, and write a little." He was also well versed in the lessons of the woods. When he was twenty-one, Boone married seventeen-year-old Rebecca Bryan. No pictures of her exist, but people described her as tall and buxom, with jet-black hair and dark eyes. She had four children by the age of twenty and ten children overall. Later, she also raised six other children whose mother had died. When Boone left on his long hunting trips, Rebecca tended the crops and kept the family going; she probably never learned to read or write. Her efforts allowed Boone to travel to Kentucky to hunt and procure furs. He wore his long hair in Indian-style braids and dressed much like the Native Americans did. Once he spent months alone in Kentucky, perhaps the only European in the whole area. When a friend asked him if he had ever gotten lost, Boone answered that he had not but admitted that he had once been "pretty confused" for several days. Another time, some so-called Long Hunters in search of furs heard a strange sound and, when they investigated, found Boone lying on his back in the middle of a field, singing loudly. Boone loved nature and the openness of Kentucky.

During Boone's first attempt to establish a settlement, some Indians killed one of his sons, and a sad Boone turned back. The next time he came, he had been hired by Richard Henderson to set up a fort. Henderson's Transylvania Company had bought a large part of Kentucky from the Indians and wanted people to settle that land. (Later,

Artist's rendering of when Daniel Boone first viewed "the beautiful level of Kentucke." (Courtesy of the Anschutz Collection)

Henderson's land claim would be rejected.) Boone led a group through the Cumberland Gap, and they blazed a trail, later called the Wilderness Road, to the place where they built Fort Boonesborough on the Kentucky River.

Daniel Walker was one of the men accompanying Boone at the time, and he later described what they felt when they saw what Boone called "the beautiful level of Kentucke" (sometime later, the name would be spelled with a *y* instead of an *e* at the end). Said Walker: "A new sky and strange earth seemed to be presented to our view. So rich a soil we had never seen before. . . . We felt ourselves at a garden where [there] was no forbidden fruit." Two days later, however, reality struck. Indians killed two men in the group, one black and one white, and wounded Walker during the attack. The group suspended their travels for twelve days to allow Walker to heal (although some of his friends expected him to die). He lived, and they eventually went on to set up Fort Boonesborough.

Once the three forts at Harrodsburg, Boonesborough, and Stanford had been set up, other people started to arrive, but it was neither an easy trip nor an easy time.

Hard Times

William Whitley and his family left Virginia for Kentucky in the same year that the early forts were built. He told of going through the wilderness: "At times my wife would fall, horse & all, & at other times she and her children [were] all in a file tied together, for where one went, all must go. In that situation, we were 33 days in the wilderness. . . . Had rain, hail, and snow with the disadvantages large." They made it through safely, however, and Whitley and his wife, Esther, built what has been called the first brick home in Kentucky. It still stands in Lincoln County. He died at the age of sixty-five, fighting for his country in the War of 1812. Soon after his death, Kentucky named a county in his honor.

Seven-year-old Sarah Graham came to Kentucky five years after the Whitleys arrived. Later, when someone asked about that trip, she noted that she had come with 300 other people. The large group managed to avoid Indian attacks, but she recalled seeing parts of bodies in the bushes around her, left from other fights. After the group got to Kentucky, Simon Kenton visited, and she remembered talking with him. One of Sarah Graham's enduring memories concerned another young girl she saw there. The girl had been badly injured in an Indian attack, and when her father came for her, she could not see him clearly because of the blood and yelled out, "Indians! Indians!" Her father kissed her and comforted her and held her in his arms. She lived for only a few more days. Sarah Graham lived for many years, in Mercer and Bath counties in Kentucky. But she never forgot what she had seen as a young girl.

Josiah Collins came to Boonesborough a few years after its construction and fought in several battles with Boone and Harrod. But peaceful activities, such as teaching school, could be violent too. Collins told the story of a Lexington teacher named John McKinney and what he saw at school one day: "He looked round and saw a wild cat sitting in the door and picked up a ruler to throw at it. As he turned, the cat sprung into his arms and seized him with its teeth. . . . Some [people] came in to his help, alarmed by his screams. The cat was killed." The teacher lived, but after that, people called him "Wildcat" McKinney. Danger lurked everywhere in frontier Kentucky.

All those settlers and many more faced hardship and pain, yet they survived. They cried for the dead, but they went on living. Such courage helped shape a state.

Choices

During the time of Kentucky's settlement, people began to think of themselves more and more as Americans and less and less as English, Irish, or some other European nationality. Kentucky settlement took place during the American Revolutionary War. The area became a battleground in that conflict, and people in the region had to choose which side to support. They had to make other hard choices as well.

Ten days after the Declaration of Independence was signed in far-off Philadelphia, Daniel Boone's thirteen-year-old daughter Jemima and two Callaway girls—Betsy, age sixteen, and Fanny, age twelve—got into a boat near Boonesborough, to escape the fort's walls and enjoy the cool river water. Daniel Boone related what happened next: "In July 14, 1776 two of Col. Callaway's daughters and one of mine having strolled across the Kentucky River in search of wild flowers, were made prisoners by some Indians." When the leader of the small group of Native Americans found out he had seized Jemima, he remarked, "We have done pretty well for old Boone this time." Quickly, a group from Boonesborough was organized to go after the girls. The young captives helped by leaving a trail—breaking branches along the way, digging their heels into the ground to leave marks, or tearing off small pieces of clothing. But

This is the only painting of Daniel Boone created while he was alive. Photographs did not become common until the 1840s. (Courtesy of the Massachusetts Historical Society)

Boone and the other rescuers soon faced a hard choice. The rescue party could continue to follow the trail, but the Indians had a big lead, and the settlers might not catch them before they crossed the Ohio River into safety. The other choice would be to leave the trail, take a shortcut, and catch up with the Indians. Boone thought he knew where the Native Americans were heading, but if he was wrong, the girls might never be rescued. Following the trail seemed to be the safer choice, but doing so might lead to failure. A man in the rescue party later described what Boone did: "Paying no further attention to the trail, he now took a straight course through the woods, with increased speed, followed by the men in perfect silence." Boone's risky choice worked. They caught the Indians in Bath County and wounded two of them; the other three escaped. The girls were not harmed, and when everyone was safe, they all sat down and cried with joy. Boone's choice had been the right one.

Later, when Daniel Boone was wounded defending Boonesborough, Simon Kenton carried him back toward the fort. Jemima Boone—the daughter that Daniel had saved from the Indians—ran out to help bring her father to safety.

A year and a half after that attack, Daniel Boone faced another hard choice. He and 27 men had gone to get salt from the briny water that seeped out of the ground at a salt lick. The settlers needed salt to preserve their meat, since they had no way to keep it cool for very long. While at the salt lick, the men were surrounded by 120 Indians. Boone knew that although his men could fight, they could not defeat such a large force and would likely be killed. Boone made his choice and told them to surrender, although many of the men disagreed with that decision. The Native Americans took Boone and the others into Ohio, where Boone faced Chief Blackfish. The chief asked Boone if he had killed Blackfish's son in an earlier battle. Boone admitted his responsibility and then added, "But many things happen in war best forgotten." The Indians admired courage, and Chief Blackfish said, "Brave man. When we in war you kill me. I kill you. All right." He accepted Boone into the tribe as a replacement for his son and called him *Shel-Tow-y* or "Big Turtle." Boone lived with the Native Americans for four months, but when he heard them making plans to attack Boonesborough, he escaped to warn the people at the fort and help them prepare for the attack. When the siege came, it went on for eleven days. The Indians tried to tunnel under the fort walls, but

Kentucky Lives: Simon Kenton

Simon Kenton could have been as famous as Daniel Boone, but no one wrote about Kenton's exploits. His career was almost as important as Boone's, and once he even saved Boone's life. But Kenton was largely forgotten for a long time.

Kenton was born in Virginia and never learned to read or write. At age sixteen, he got in a fight and thought he had killed his opponent, so he changed his name to Simon Butler and fled to what is now Maysville, Kentucky. There, he planted the first corn grown by settlers north of the Kentucky River.

The tall, strong man helped protect the new settlements. In the process, he was captured by the Shawnee, tied on a horse, and run through briars and branches in the woods. Once he lived through that experience, the Indians made him run the gauntlet: two rows of armed Native Americans lined up, and he had to run between them as they hit him. Many of those forced to run the gauntlet did not survive, but Simon did. Before he finally escaped, he was made to run the gauntlet again and was almost burned at the stake.

After Simon got back to Kentucky, he discovered that the man he thought he had killed was alive. So he took back his old name and continued to explore in places where others would not go. One man to whom Kenton owed money decided not to try to collect it. He wrote: "Too dangerous to go where Kenton is."

Later Kenton married and settled down. He and his wife had four children, but she died in a fire. He then married her first cousin, and they had five more children. Kenton moved to Ohio but later returned to Kentucky as an old man. Authorities jailed him for nonpayment of a debt, but they released the old pioneer the next year.

Kenton died in Ohio in 1836, a forgotten hero in a distant land. Four years later, Kentucky named a county in his honor.

the wet ground caused the tunnel to collapse. Finally, the Indians left, and the fort was still standing.

Sometimes, choices made for the wrong reasons have disastrous results. A case in point is the Battle of Blue Licks, which took place in 1782. It has been called the last battle of the Revolutionary War. Some Native Americans and a few English soldiers attacked Bryan's Station, near Lexington—the biggest fort in Kentucky. They quickly abandoned the attack, but settlers from other forts joined together to pursue them.

They caught up with the fleeing English and Indians at Blue Licks, but Daniel Boone warned the army that the Indians might be lying in wait to ambush them. Another man who was eager to fight yelled out, "Them that ain't cowards, follow me." The men followed, and Boone sadly said, "Come on, we are all slaughtered men." Boone had been right—it was a trap. With twice as many men, the Indians and the English struck the American force. At least sixty-six Americans died there—one-third of those involved. In the middle of the attack, Boone told his son Israel to get on a horse and ride away, but Israel said, "Father, I won't leave you." He was killed. Boone managed to escape. It was the worst defeat the settlers experienced. But it was also the last major Indian battle in the state. A state park now occupies the site.

The End of the Frontier

As more people moved into Kentucky, and as the Indian threat faded, the settlers' need for these leaders diminished. They remembered the courageous acts of the early frontiersmen but wanted a new type of leader now. James Harrod went on a hunting trip and disappeared. Simon Kenton moved to Ohio. Daniel Boone left for Missouri.

The early pioneers had helped settle, or resettle, the land. But in doing that, they also did away with what had brought them there in the first place—the wild animals, the free land, and more. They destroyed the wilderness. In 1820—the year Boone died—the last of what had once been thousands of buffalo was seen in Kentucky, in Hart County. Of those billions of passenger pigeons that had once flown over, all were gone from Kentucky by 1899. Fifteen years later, the last one on earth died. Like the early pioneers, they passed from the scene.

The new American nation emerged at the same time as Kentucky. The country wanted a hero who represented the "common man," and Daniel Boone became that symbol, standing for all those people who had risked their lives to come and settle in Kentucky. In that way, his fame extended to all of them.

Statehood

George Rogers Clark served as a bridge from the pioneers to the new leaders. Tall, red-headed, with a hot temper, Clark was only in his twen-

ties when he led armies north of the Ohio River to try to keep the Indians and the English soldiers away. In a truly heroic march, his men took
forts from the English; later, other soldiers raided Native American villages as well. Many people credited Clark's victories with bringing that
area into the new American nation after the Revolutionary War. But he
was not as successful in times of peace. Like Harrod, Kenton, Logan, and
others, he did not receive enough praise.

Clark and many of the early settlers on that first frontier had come
from Virginia. At the time, Kentucky constituted part of Virginia, and it
consisted of only one county. Later, it divided into several counties but
remained part of Virginia. During the Revolutionary War, as the nation sought freedom, Kentuckians asked for statehood. They based it on
"that spark, which kindled the flame of Liberty."

Finally, on June 1, 1792, Kentucky became the fifteenth state in the
new United States and the first state west of the mountains. The people
chose as their first governor a man named Isaac Shelby. Of medium
height and only a fair speaker, the forty-one-year-old Shelby was originally from Maryland; he had been a war hero and moved to Lincoln
County, Kentucky, at the end of the conflict. He started out from Danville that June day, with horsemen around him, and headed for the temporary capital at Lexington. When he arrived, people fired rifles and
cannon in the air to honor him. Then he took the oath of office as governor. Three days later, legislators met in a two-story log cabin. One of
the first orders of business was to decide where the permanent capital
would be located. Groups of people from various towns vied for that
honor, but Frankfort made the best offer. It promised land in town to
build on, money for construction, and building materials—glass, nails,
locks, stone, and timber. The new state had a new capital and now faced
a new future.

What of those people who had lived for thousands of years in what
was now the state of Kentucky? What happened to the Native Americans? By the time of statehood, most of them had been driven well beyond the borders of Kentucky. The last large group of Indians passed
through the state much later, however, in 1838. But they did not do
so voluntarily. The United States forced some 16,000 members of the
Cherokee Nation on a 1,200-mile journey to their new home, on lands
far away. Thousands of men, women, and children went through such
towns as Hopkinsville, Princeton, and Paducah in the cold of winter,

Trail of Tears. (Courtesy of the Woolaroc Museum)

on the frozen roads. One-quarter of the Native Americans forced from their homes did not survive the trip; some 4,000 perished. The tribe called it *Nunna-Da-Ul-Tsun-Y,* or "the place where they cried." Others termed it the Trail of Tears.

The last, brief, major Indian presence in Kentucky was gone. But the frontier had ended long before that.

CHAPTER THREE

Different Kentuckys

The People of Kentucky

Kentucky is now home to more than 4 million people. That puts it exactly in the middle of all the states in terms of population. But that ranking has varied greatly over the years. Soon after Kentucky became a state, about 221,000 men, women, and children lived there. It grew very rapidly at first. In fact, by 1840, Kentucky had become the sixth most populous state in the nation. Since then, however, other states have grown faster.

Who are the people who now live in Kentucky? Officially, 91 percent of Kentuckians are white, 7 percent are black, and 2 percent are from other backgrounds—Asian, Indian, or other. People of Hispanic origin account for about 2 percent of Kentuckians.

The United States has been called a nation of immigrants, because everyone who settled here was originally from someplace else—mostly Europe, Asia, or Africa. The new immigrants arriving in Kentucky now are doing exactly what other immigrants have done for hundreds of years. They are making a new home in Kentucky.

Two hundred years ago, Kentucky had a more varied population than it does now. After all, everyone in the new state was likely an immigrant or the child of an immigrant. At that time, 19 percent of Kentuckians were African American. The rest came from European backgrounds; about 52 percent of those from Europe had family ties to England, some 25 percent were from Scotland or Northern Ireland, 9 percent were Irish, nearly 7 percent were Welsh, and 5 percent were German.

When Kentucky first became a state, people spoke a number of languages and with many accents. A few Africans still used their native tongues, as did the Germans. Even those speaking English might have heavy Irish or Scottish accents. About fifty years after statehood, a large number of German and Irish immigrants came to Kentucky and settled mostly in the cities on the Ohio River. In Covington in Kenton County,

Kentucky Lives: Population, 1800–2000

1800—220,955	1920—2,416,630
1820—564,135	1940—2,845,627
1840—779,828	1960—3,038,156
1860—1,155,684	1980—3,660,324
1880—1,648,690	2000—4,041,769
1900—2,147,174	

for example, more than one-fourth of the people had been born in another country. The same held true in Louisville. A variety of languages could be heard in frontier and pre–Civil War Kentucky.

Kentucky Homes

Where do Kentuckians live? For most of the state's history, they lived in rural areas, and in fact, almost half of all people in Kentucky still reside in such places. The state remains much more rural than the nation as a whole.

When asked where they live, many Kentuckians who live outside the main cities answer not with the name of a town or city but with the name of a county. Kentucky has many counties—120 in all—which is more counties than any other state except for Texas and Georgia. This means that some counties are very small. In physical size, Pike County has the most land and Gallatin County the least. In population, the smallest is Robertson County, which had only 2,266 people in the year 2000. The largest in population is Jefferson County (which includes Louisville) with 693,604. One in every six Kentucky counties has fewer than 10,000 people. In some rural areas, no large towns exist, so counties are the places that people call home.

The state legislature created some counties for good reasons and some for not-so-good ones. In the past, when travel was slow, a new county might have been established because people lived too far from the county seat. Sometimes legislators created a new county to honor a person. Other counties divided into two because the people living there did not get along with one another. The last county in Kentucky was formed about a century ago. Some people consider 120 counties too many, but all agree that it would be very hard to reduce the number now by combining counties.

The Land

The geography of Kentucky shaped the land and its history, just as the people did. In frontier times, for instance, the mountains forced people to travel through the Cumberland Gap or down the Ohio River. Other physical features have shaped the state in various ways as well.

In size, Kentucky is not a large state. It contains 40,395 square miles and ranks thirty-seventh among the fifty states in area. It has a good location, near the center of the nation, and many of the largest cities in America are close to Kentucky.

Kentucky can be described as a fairly long and narrow state. Traveling from one end to the other, from easternmost Pike County to westernmost Fulton County, would require a 458-mile trip. Going from north to south, at the widest point, would require a trip of 171 miles. The highest point in the state is Big Black Mountain in Harlan County, at a height of 4,145 feet. The lowest point is on the Mississippi River, where Kentucky drops to 237 feet above sea level. There, Kentucky touches one of the seven states that surround it.

Most of Kentucky's border had already been determined by the time it became a state. Much of that border follows waterways. In fact, it is the only state that has rivers creating three sides of its boundary—the Mississippi in the west, the Ohio in the north, and the Big Sandy and Tug Fork in the east. Mountains and a survey line complete the state borders.

Rivers do more than create Kentucky's borders. As a state, it has more navigable streams and rivers than any other state except Alaska. Major rivers include the Ohio, Cumberland, Tennessee, Mississippi, Kentucky, Green, Licking, and others. In the early days, rivers provided an easy means of travel and a way to take farm goods to market as well. Rivers provided water for people, crops, and animals, and towns and cities grew up near them as a result. Those early rivers have changed over time, as dams have been built for flood control and recreation, creating large lakes in some places. Rivers still remain important for Kentuckians.

Kentucky counties, 1920 to present. (Map by Dick Gilbreath)

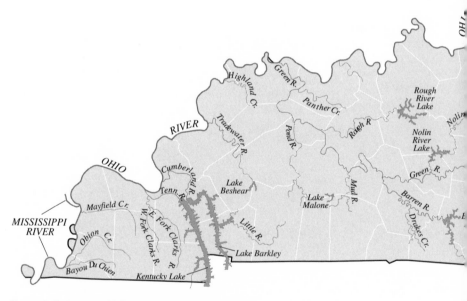

Kentucky's rivers and lakes. (Map by Dick Gilbreath)

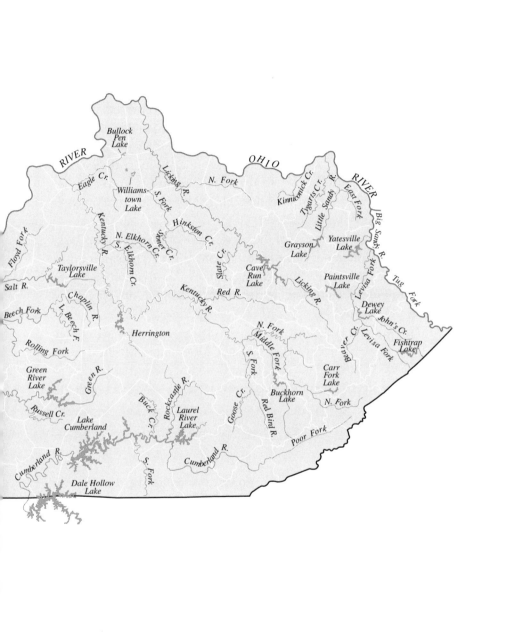

RIVER

Bullock
Pen
Lake

OHIO

Eagle Cr.

Williams-
town
Lake

Licking R.

N. Fork

Kinniconick Cr.

Tygarts Cr.

Little Sandy R.

East Fork

RIVER

Big Sandy R.

Floyd Fork

Kentucky R.

S. Fork

Hinkston Cr.

Grayson
Lake

Yatesville
Lake

N. Elkhorn

Stoner Cr.

Taylorsville
Lake

S. Elkhorn

Elkhorn Cr.

Slate Cr.

Cave
Run
Lake

Paintsville
Lake

Levisa Fork

Tug Fork

Salt R.

Kentucky R.

Red R.

Licking R.

Chaplin R.

L. Beech F.

Beech Fork

Herrington

Dewey
Lake

John's Cr.

Rolling Fork

N. Fork

Middle Fork

Beaver Cr.

Levisa Fork

Fishtrap
Lake

Green
River
Lake

Green R.

S. Fork

Carr
Fork
Lake

Russell Cr.

Buck Cr.

Rockcastle R.

Laurel
River
Lake

Goose Cr.

Red Bird R.

Buckhorn
Lake

N. Fork

Poor Fork

Lake
Cumberland

Cumberland R.

S. Fork

Cumberland R.

Dale Hollow
Lake

Rivers have not always been friendly to the people of the state, however. During the great flood of 1937, water covered many Kentucky towns when rain fell for almost three full days. The Ohio River rose fifty-seven feet higher than its usual level. That 1937 flood caused problems for cities all along the rivers. At Covington, water covered a third of the city. The flood affected six of every ten houses in Louisville, and people rode boats down Main Street. Thousands left their water-covered and mud-filled homes. At Paducah, almost the whole city lay submerged. It looked like a ghost town. Water covered smaller towns all along the Ohio River. At Lewisport in Hancock County, 151 of the homes had floodwater in them; only 17 did not. The Kentucky River flooded more than half of Frankfort, making it necessary to remove the prisoners from the state penitentiary to keep them from drowning. All over Kentucky, people lost almost everything they owned.

But it was two years later that the greatest loss of life took place. Walls of water from flash floods rushed through Breathitt and Rowan counties in the eastern part of the state, leaving a path of destruction and some eighty people dead. Floods still remain a threat for parts of Kentucky, as evidenced by one in 1997.

On the opposite end of the weather spectrum, droughts have created hard times as well. During a 1930 drought, for example, Mayfield in the western part of the state had no rain for a month. Across the area, crops died, and the green bluegrass turned brown. Nature gives life, and it can take it away.

Climate

Due to its location, Kentucky has a moderate or temperate climate, with four distinct seasons. It usually does not have the extreme cold and deep snow of the far northern states or the high heat of the Deep South. Temperatures seldom go below 0 or above 100 degrees. Snowfall amounts are generally small. Overall, rainfall and snowfall total about forty-five inches per year.

Within the state, differences in climate exist. For example, temperatures in Northern Kentucky tend to be about five degrees cooler than those in West Kentucky. A place such as Somerset, in the south-central part of the state, may get ten more inches of rain per year than Covington, to the north. Average temperatures for the whole state range from the low thirties in January to the high seventies in July. Kentucky's climate allows a growing season of seven to eight months each year.

Geographic Regions

Geographers often divide Kentucky into five (or six) regions—Jackson Purchase, Pennyroyal (or Pennyrile), Western Coal Fields, Bluegrass, and Mountains (or Eastern Coal Fields). A very small region, called the Knobs, is now usually included in the Bluegrass.

Jackson Purchase

The Jackson Purchase is the newest and smallest region of Kentucky. In 1818, twenty-six years after Kentucky became a state, former Kentucky governor Isaac Shelby and future U.S. president Andrew Jackson bought the land from the Chickasaw Indians for the United States. They paid the Native Americans $300,000, with payments to be spread over fifteen years. It was called the Jackson Purchase. Out of that area, Kentucky created eight counties.

The Mississippi, Ohio, and Tennessee rivers form the borders of the Jackson Purchase on three sides. Within the Purchase, a very small piece of land is separated from the rest of the state by the waters of the Mississippi River and can be reached only by going into Tennessee. That region is called New Madrid Bend. Overall, the Jackson Purchase area is the lowest part of Kentucky and has a lot of flat, fertile, river-bottom land. This part of Kentucky sits closest to the New Madrid Fault Line, where huge earthquakes occurred in 1811 and 1812. When they ended, a new lake had been formed. Water filled a great crack in the earth and created Reelfoot Lake in Tennessee and in Fulton County, Kentucky.

Kentucky Voices

Near Kentucky is New Madrid, Missouri. Over several months in 1811 and 1812, it became the epicenter of perhaps the greatest earthquake in the nation's history. The shocks hit Kentucky very hard. Hundreds of miles away, walls cracked. Tremors caused bells to ring in churches as far away as Boston, Massachusetts. The Mississippi River flowed backward briefly. ▶

Luckily, western Kentucky was not heavily populated at the time, so not many people died. Scientists believe that another earthquake will occur in that area sometime in the future.

One man who was in the area at the time of the quake described what he saw:

We felt the shock of an earthquake, accompanied by a rumbling noise, resembling the distant firing of a cannon. . . . The river . . . was boiling, foaming, and roaring terrifically. Men, women, and children gave up in despair, some fainting, so great was their fear. . . . The earth was in continual agitation, visibly waving as a gentle sea.

A few months later, another man wrote about the aftermath:

The surface of the ground was cracked in almost every direction and stood like yawning gulfs, so wide I could scarcely leap over them. [On] the shores of the river, the banks were cracked, trees broken off, and in many places acres of ground sunk down so that the tops of the trees just appeared above the surface of the water. All nature appeared in ruins.

Pennyroyal (or Pennyrile)

The largest physical region of Kentucky is named for a small plant. More than one-fourth of Kentucky's counties lie in this region. Probably the best-known natural feature of the Pennyroyal is Mammoth Cave, the longest underground cave system in the world. So far, explorers have discovered some 340 miles of caverns. It became a U.S. national park in 1941. This cave and others in the area were created out of limestone rock. Water flowed through cracks in the rock over a very long time, forming open places. Later, the water drained away, leaving the spectacular caves.

Western Coal Fields

This region got its name from the coal that lies under its surface. The mostly level land also offers good farming. Several rivers run through the Western Coal Fields as well.

Bluegrass

Kentucky is called the Bluegrass State because of the bluegrass that grows in this region. Bluegrass is not native to Kentucky, however, and despite its name, it is really a dark green. People brought the grass from England, and by the time Daniel Boone arrived, it had already spread. Now, all over the world, people call it Kentucky bluegrass. It helped make the region a good place for animals, because horses and cows graze on it.

The physical Bluegrass region has rich farmland, rolling hills, and deep gorges on the Kentucky River. The outer parts have more hills, called the Knobs.

Mountains (Eastern Coal Fields)

This region, one of the largest in Kentucky, is part of a mountain chain that stretches from Georgia in the south to New York in the north. The highest parts of Kentucky are located here. The forest-covered hills in the area do not leave much level land in the "hollows." Many state parks and a national forest have been created in the region because of its scenic beauty. Natural Bridge, a rock formation high on a hill, lies close to Red River Gorge, which also offers scenery and hiking.

This rock formation, created thousands of years ago by the forces of nature, is located in Natural Bridge State Park in Powell County. (Courtesy of the Kentucky Department of Travel)

Cumberland Falls. (Photograph by Thomas G. Barnes)

One of the noteworthy physical features of Kentucky is Cumberland Falls on the Cumberland River in Whitley County. On certain nights, something special happens there. As the water goes over the falls, the light from the full moon creates a moonbow, the nighttime version of a rainbow. It is the only moonbow in the Western Hemisphere.

The other important natural feature here is coal. It is taken from the earth through deep underground mines or through strip mining, which removes the dirt and takes the coal from the surface.

Cultural or Human Regions

Perhaps a better way to understand Kentucky is to divide it into regions in a different way. The geographic regions are based on the natural or physical features of the state, but if you ask people where they live, that is not how they answer. People are more likely to say that they live in Northern Kentucky than in the Bluegrass. Those who live in the Penny-royal region think of themselves as living in West Kentucky. So, looking at it this way, Kentucky has seven cultural areas—Appalachia (or Eastern Kentucky), Northern Kentucky, the Bluegrass, South-Central Kentucky, Louisville, West Kentucky, and Jackson Purchase.

Appalachia (Eastern Kentucky)

Because the Appalachian Mountains cover the eastern part of the state, some people call that area Appalachia. Others simply refer to it as Eastern Kentucky. Either way, it is a place of hills and mountains, with few large cities. Only two towns have populations exceeding 10,000—Ashland and Middlesboro. Towns about half that size are London, Corbin, Williamsburg, Pikeville, Hazard, and Morehead.

More than any other region of the state, Eastern Kentucky has been shaped by its past, by its geography, and by writers from outside the area. Eastern Kentucky was one of the last parts of the state to be settled, due in part to the hilly terrain. Slowly, people began to move in because the eastern part of the state had good hunting, good water, and good land in the valleys. These settlers had small farms, just like elsewhere in Kentucky. Over the years, however, the region became cut off from the rest of the state and did not grow as much. Some bitter feuds were started, the most famous being the Hatfield-McCoy feud in Pike County. Many others raged for years, and hundreds of people died. At that time, more than a century ago, Appalachian stereotypes developed when people from outside the region came in and wrote stories about the land and its people and then made films about it. Although their depiction of Appa-

---

Kentucky Voices

Kentuckians view themselves in various ways, as these documents, written over a period of 150 years, show.

1828: "My dear honeys, heaven is a Kentucky of a place." (*The Christian Traveller*)

1915: "Daughter of the East, Mother of West / Link that binds North and South." (quoted in Josiah Combs, *All that Is Kentucky*)

1929: "No matter how far or how long her children roam, once a Kentuckian, always a Kentuckian." (Lorine L. Butler, *My Old Kentucky Home*)

1938: "Kentuckians are different." (M. B. Morton, *Kentuckians Are Different*)

1976: "I live here in Ohio, and I'll die here. But I want my wife to put on my tombstone: 'Here lies Stanley, but he'd rather be in Kentucky.'" (quoted in Wade Hall, *The Kentucky Book*, 1979)

lachians as poor "hillbillies" ignored much of reality, once the stereotype emerged, the region found it difficult to overcome that image.

At about the same time, the region started to change. People began mining coal in large amounts, and almost overnight, quiet farmland became coal camps. As people left their farms to dig coal and others moved into the region for the same purpose, the population drastically increased. Coal mining is no longer as vital to the region's economy as it once was. Tourists who visit the many scenic areas have made Appalachia more important than ever. Still, to many people, Appalachia means coal.

Northern Kentucky

The three counties of Campbell, Kenton, and Boone and the smaller rural counties around them form Northern Kentucky. For a long time, the people there tended to feel more connected to Cincinnati, Ohio, across the river, than to Kentucky. In fact, the Cincinnati and Northern Kentucky International Airport is located in Kentucky and is the largest airport in the state.

Once, Newport and Covington stood as the second and third largest cities in the state. But the area grew slowly during much of the twentieth century, and first Lexington and then other cities passed them in size. Recently, however, Northern Kentucky has become one of the growth areas of the state. The cities of Florence, Fort Thomas, Erlanger, Independence, and Burlington have joined Covington and Newport as cities with more than 10,000 people. Now Northern Kentucky is considered an area unto itself, rather than just a part of Cincinnati. Northern Kentucky University and Thomas More College attract students to their halls of learning. The region has also become the North American headquarters for Toyota and the national center for Ashland Oil.

Northern Kentucky forms part of what has been called the Golden Triangle of Kentucky, where most of the state's recent growth has taken place. At the points of the triangle are Lexington, Louisville, and Covington.

Bluegrass

A circle stretching forty miles in all directions from the core of Lexington would include most of the Bluegrass. Cities with populations exceeding

10,000 include Richmond, Frankfort, Nicholasville, Georgetown, Winchester, and Danville.

Because people settled this part of Kentucky first, it includes many historic places. In Danville, the state's founders discussed statehood and started the process. At Frankfort, the Old State Capitol still stands, a beautiful testament to the place where people conducted the business of the state for eighty years. Rebuilt forts at Harrodsburg and Boonesborough remind visitors of the frontier. Also near Harrodsburg is Shaker Village of Pleasant Hill, where a religious group lived and worked in the now-quiet buildings and grounds. Cane Ridge in Bourbon County contains the church around which one of the greatest religious events in American history revolved—the Great Revival of 1801. The full story of such events can be found at the Thomas D. Clark Center for Kentucky History in Frankfort. Many old homes also dot the region, where people can walk the same floors as the leaders of long ago.

From those early times to the present, the Bluegrass has also been known for its horse farms. More than 180 years ago, someone from England wrote: "Their horses are the best in the United States." They continue to be. Racetracks such as the historic Keeneland Race Course in Lexington prove that to be true every year. The Kentucky Horse Park near Lexington tells the story of horses.

To keep horses on the farms, first Irish workers and later skilled black builders created rock fences. Some say that Kentucky has the largest number of such stone fences in the world. Later, wood plank fences replaced the stone ones on horse farms. In addition to horses, agriculture remains important on Bluegrass farms.

Most people who work in the area do not work on horse farms. Service and information industries employ large numbers—in hospitals, banks, schools, or government. In the capital at Frankfort, state workers serve all of Kentucky, while Lexington has become a center for doctors, lawyers, and bankers.

The region also has some of the oldest and best colleges and universities in Kentucky. State-supported schools include the University of Kentucky in Lexington, Kentucky State University in Frankfort, and Eastern Kentucky University in Richmond. Private colleges set up more than 175 years ago include Transylvania University in Lexington, Centre College in Danville, and Georgetown College. Several other colleges grew up later. The professors and the other professionals who work in the area make the region a highly educated part of Kentucky and one of the best educated in the nation.

Other people who work in the Bluegrass build things, from computer printers manufactured by Lexmark in Lexington to cars produced at the large Toyota plant near Georgetown. The region's central location, airport, and good interstate highways and parkways have helped it grow.

The heart of the Bluegrass remains Lexington, the second largest city in the state. For the first thirty years after Kentucky became a state, Lexington was the major city and the largest city west of the mountains for a time. That changed when steamboats made river connections crucial, because Lexington does not sit on a major river. (It is still the largest city in the eastern United States that is not on a major body of water.) As a result of the transportation changes, Lexington declined for a time; in the 1950s, however, it began to grow again, doubling in size over the next thirty years. Lexington was one of the fastest-growing cities in the nation at that time.

South-Central Kentucky

Not Eastern, West, or Bluegrass, this part of Kentucky stretches from Somerset in the east past Glasgow and Bowling Green in the west. In between those cities are small farms and major tourist places such as Lake Cumberland and Barren River State Parks. Though seldom mentioned when people speak of Kentucky, this region is just as important as any other. The largest city, Bowling Green, has become the fourth largest city in the state. There, Western Kentucky University offers higher education to people of the region, as do Campbellsville University and Lindsey Wilson College in Columbia.

Nearby Mammoth Cave brings in large numbers of visitors, and tourism has become a big industry. Just north of the Mammoth Cave area is a part of Kentucky that might be claimed by several regions. The cities of Elizabethtown and Radcliff in Hardin County and Bardstown in Nelson County could be considered part of the outer Bluegrass, part of the south-central region, or even tied to Louisville. However the people there see themselves, they have a rich history and play an important part in Kentucky.

Abraham Lincoln was born near Hodgenville, not far from Elizabethtown. Nearby, in Bardstown, is a house called Federal Hill, which

Kentucky Lives: Stephen Bishop

Born a slave, seventeen-year-old Stephen Bishop came with his owner to Mammoth Cave, where he became a guide through its dark depths. A year later, his owner sold the cave—and Bishop—to another man.

Over the next few years, Bishop became the most popular guide at the cave. A witty, self-educated man, he knew history and he knew how the cave had been formed. He also explored more of Mammoth Cave than any other person. The small but strong Bishop was the first to cross the Bottomless Pit, and he discovered many new parts of the cave. He also found some of the eyeless animals that live there in the total darkness.

Visitors to Mammoth Cave carried small lamps that burned lard or oil to cast a faint light in the huge cave. One visitor recalled "their lights chasing for a moment the shadows." Inside that natural wonder where no sun shone, no rain fell, no wind blew, and the temperature remained constant all year long, they found "a world to itself."

Stephen Bishop's own world changed when his owner died. The owner's will stipulated that Bishop be freed from slavery. Bishop had saved some money and bought land near the cave. But he tasted the fruits of freedom only briefly. Bishop died a year later, at age thirty-six, and was buried near the entrance to the cave he so loved.

some believe is the source of the state song "My Old Kentucky Home." Near Bardstown, workers produce another product that people connect with Kentucky—bourbon whiskey. The state ships bourbon all over the world.

Near Radcliff is Fort Knox, the army base best known as the place where the nation's gold is stored and guarded. Not as well known is the fact that, during World War II, some of the nation's greatest treasures were sent there for protection—the Declaration of Independence, the U.S. Constitution, Abraham Lincoln's Gettysburg Address, and more. Once the danger to them had passed, they went back to Washington, D.C.

Louisville

Louisville is by far the largest city in the state, and it has been since 1830. Part of the reason for its size lies in geography. For the entire length of the Ohio River, the only spot where boats could not pass was the Falls of the Ohio, where the river drops more than twenty feet within two miles. That is where Louisville grew up. Named for a king of France who helped America during the Revolutionary War, Louisville became the place where boats had to stop, unload their cargo, and then reload it on the other side of the falls. Later, a canal was built so that ships could go around the falls and move down the river faster. Still later, the first bridge (beyond Cincinnati) to cross the Ohio River was built at Louisville. That bridge and the railroads brought more people. By 1850, Louisville was the tenth biggest city in the United States. One of every five Kentuckians lives in or near Louisville, and it now ranks as the twenty-seventh largest U.S. city.

But perhaps Louisville is best known worldwide for something that takes place there on the first Saturday of May, an event that has occurred every year since 1875. On that day, three-year-old racehorses run in the Kentucky Derby at Churchill Downs, perhaps the world's most famous horse race. There are few horse farms in the Louisville area, but the Derby winner makes Louisville the horse capital for one Saturday a year.

Louisville is also known for other things. Much of the state's heavy industry is located there. The city is also home to the University of Louisville and the private colleges of Bellarmine and Spalding. The people of the city have many cultural events to choose from as well: museums, opera, ballet, plays, concerts, and all the other things that a large city has to offer. Many of those events take place at the Kentucky Center.

West Kentucky

West of Interstate 65 all the way to the Jackson Purchase, the western part of Kentucky is the most varied in the state. It has coal mining as well as rich farmland. The crops grown include corn, soybeans, and tobacco. The region has a big military base at Fort Campbell. It also features some of the best recreational areas in the state.

Dividing West Kentucky and the Jackson Purchase is the area known as Land between the Lakes. Dams built on the Tennessee and Cumberland rivers created the huge Lake Barkley and Kentucky Lake, where people from Kentucky and other states enjoy boating and fishing. Lakes at Rough River and Nolin River and at several smaller places

On the first Saturday in May, the world watches Churchill Downs to see which thorough-bred will win the Kentucky Derby. (Courtesy of the Kentucky Department of Travel)

offer water sports as well. A Shaker Village at South Union and a state park honoring John James Audubon at Henderson represent the region's history.

Owensboro, the largest city in the region, is third largest in the state and features an art center, museums, good barbecue, and Kentucky Wesleyan and Brescia colleges. Two-year community colleges also dot the region. Other cities with populations exceeding 10,000 include Hopkinsville, Henderson, Madisonville, and Fort Campbell.

Kentucky Lives: John James Audubon

The world-famous painter of birds and animals spent many of his best years in Kentucky. Born in Haiti to French parents, Audubon spent much of his early life in France. Later, he came to America, met the woman he would marry, and operated a store in Louisville. Three years later, he moved to Henderson, Kentucky.

Audubon lived in Kentucky for eight years, and all four of his children were born in the state. He and his wife, Lucy, called those years in Kentucky the happiest of their lives. Audubon spent much of his time in the woods, where he painted the fine bird portraits that would make him famous.

Audubon was a better artist than a businessman. His stores failed, and he briefly went to jail for not paying his bills. The Audubons were almost penniless when they left Kentucky. Finally, Audubon sailed to England, where his pictures were printed in beautiful color in his great work *The Birds of America*. That won him fame, respect, and wealth.

Audubon died in New York, and his widow moved back to Kentucky to be with her sister-in-law in Shelbyville. She died there. John James Audubon's legacy includes the Audubon State Park and Museum in Henderson and, most of all, his paintings.

Jackson Purchase

The Jackson Purchase came to be part of Kentucky later and in a different way from other parts of the state, and its land patterns and even its roads reflect its distinct origins. Also, the people who settled there came north out of Tennessee, whereas the rest of western Kentucky was populated mostly by people moving from other parts of Kentucky.

The three largest cities are Paducah, Mayfield, and Murray, home of Murray State University. Resort parks at Kenlake and Kentucky Dam Village bring tourists to the region. Many people attend the annual picnic at the small town of Fancy Farm in Graves County, which attracts political leaders from all over the state who come to talk to voters.

Regionalism

What does it mean for Kentucky and its people that the state has so many counties and several regions? On the plus side, it gives the people

---

Kentucky Lives: Bobbie Ann Mason

Where you are born can influence your life in many ways. Bobbie Ann Mason was born in Mayfield in western Kentucky. She grew up on a farm and became the first person in her family to go to college. Mason later taught at a college herself but did not like it. What she wanted to do was to write stories about Kentucky. Success did not come easily, however. Nineteen times she submitted articles to magazines, and nineteen times she was turned down. She persevered, and on the twentieth try, the magazine accepted her work and printed it. She was forty years old at the time. Mason has since written many prize-winning books, including *In Country,* which was made into a motion picture starring Bruce Willis. Almost all her books are based on her western Kentucky background, telling the stories of rural, small-town, working-class people.

Bobbie Ann Mason said that she left Mayfield because "I wanted to go places and see the world." Although she traveled a lot, she never forgot the things that shaped her. She said, "We're free to roam, because we've always known where home is." Finally, she did come home again. She and her husband live in Anderson County, Kentucky, where Mason continues to write the books that help Kentuckians and others understand who they are.

---

a sense of belonging and makes them feel like a part of the land. On the minus side, it means that there are many Kentuckys, not just one. Each county and each region is different, and those distinctions mean that the citizens of Kentucky have to work very hard to live and work together.

Covington, in Northern Kentucky, is actually closer to Canada than it is to the westernmost part of the state. Pikeville, in the east, is nearer to the Atlantic Ocean than it is to the far parts of the Jackson Purchase. Students at Murray State University in the west live closer to the University of Mississippi than to the University of Kentucky. Towns and areas outside the Golden Triangle may feel that they do not get enough attention. Kentucky has to make a special effort to live up to the first part of its motto: "United we stand; divided we fall."

Kentucky Names

In counties and regions all across Kentucky, small towns have unusual names. Some of the oddest names are:

Monkey's Eyebrow (Ballard County)
Eighty-Eight (Barren County)
Bugtussle (Monroe County)
Mousie (Knott County)
Whoopflarea (Owsley County)

There are also towns in Kentucky with the same names as cities in foreign countries. Kentucky has a Moscow, a Paris, a London, a Cadiz, an Athens, a Versailles, and a Berlin, for example (although locals may pronounce the names differently). By whatever name and in whatever region, Kentucky places are very special to the people who live there.

CHAPTER FOUR

The Government of Kentucky

The treasurer of Kentucky receives the tax monies paid by Kentucky citizens to operate the state. In 1888, the treasurer left his office and did not return. People last recalled seeing him stuffing money in a sack. It turned out that he had been stealing the state's money. He had been the state treasurer for twenty years, and the unsuspecting people had called him "Honest Dick" Tate. He was not honest, however, and his actions had an effect on how the state was run for more than 100 years. It also remains one of the state's mysteries, with some answers provided at the end of the chapter.

The Kentucky Constitution

When Kentucky became a state on June 1, 1792, it wrote its own state constitution. That document started out by identifying who was behind the formation of the new state: "We, the people of the commonwealth of Kentucky."

Kentucky Voices

The Congress of the United States agreed to Kentucky's statehood in a law that was passed in February 1791 but did not go into effect until June 1792. It said:

That the Congress doth consent that the said district of Kentucky be formed into a new state, separate from and independent of, the said Commonwealth of Virginia.

And be it further enacted, that the State of Kentucky shall be received and admitted into this Union, as a new and entire member of the United States of America.

Only four states call themselves commonwealths. Why does Kentucky? Actually, there is no real legal difference between a commonwealth and a state. Virginia called itself a commonwealth (based on certain events connected to England), and since Kentucky had once been part of Virginia, it simply called itself a commonwealth as well.

That first constitution made it clear who had the final right to make decisions in Kentucky: "All power is inherent in the people." For the late eighteenth century, Kentucky's first constitution seemed very liberal in some ways. In almost all the other states, people had to own land or pay a certain amount of rent in order to vote. From statehood, Kentuckians could vote whether they owned land or not.

At first, only white men voted. Slaves could not vote, nor could women. Finally, after much struggle, all citizens—black and white, male and female—won the right to vote. In 1955, Kentucky gave eighteen-year-olds the right to vote, but the nation did not follow suit until sixteen years later. Again, the commonwealth had been a national leader.

Kentucky's voting practices have changed in other ways over the years. In addition to who can vote, how they vote has been transformed. For a long time, when election time came, people could vote over a three-day period rather than on one day, as now. Voters would stand before officials and tell them out loud how they wanted to vote—called voice voting. Everyone nearby would know how an individual voted. Later, voting became secret, with each voter placing a paper ballot in a box. Again, Kentucky led the nation in making that change. Currently, the state uses electronic voting machines.

In a broader way, Kentucky's constitutions have changed as well. That first one lasted only seven years before new ideas made it necessary to write a second one in 1799. A third followed a half century later. Kentucky's fourth constitution, which was adopted in 1891, still remains in force, although many amendments have modified it significantly over the years.

Levels and Branches of Government

Government exists at three different levels—local, state, and national. Early in the state's history, citizens dealt mostly with local government. Other levels of government usually affected them only when they paid their taxes, went to the post office, or voted. Later, as state and national governments began to offer many more services, they began to have an almost daily impact on the lives of Kentuckians.

As in the nation, Kentucky has three state-level branches of government—executive, judicial, and legislative. Perhaps the best way to examine how each branch operates in the commonwealth is simply to go into the Kentucky state capitol building and start there. The capitol, which was opened for use in 1909, is almost 403 feet long and 180 feet wide. Many consider it one of the most beautiful state capitols in the nation.

The Executive Branch

On the first floor of Kentucky's capitol resides the executive branch of government. It includes some elected statewide offices, such as the attorney general and the secretary of state, but the governor is the most important person in the executive branch.

To be governor of Kentucky, a person must be at least thirty years old, must have lived in the state for six years, must be elected by the people, and must take the oath of office. Kentucky's present constitution ini-

Kentucky's beautiful capitol building is the center of state government. (Courtesy of the Kentucky Office of Creative Services)

Kentucky Voices

The oath of office taken by the governor was written into the 1891 Kentucky Constitution (note the outdated section on dueling). It reads:

I do solemnly swear that I will support the Constitution of the United States and the Constitution of this Commonwealth, and be faithful and true to the Commonwealth of Kentucky as long as I continue to be a citizen thereof, and that I will faithfully execute, to the best of my ability, the office of governor according to law; and I further solemnly swear that since the adoption of the present Constitution, I, being a citizen of this State, have not fought a duel with deadly weapons within this state nor out of it, nor have I sent or accepted a challenge to fight a duel with deadly weapons, nor have I acted as second in carrying a challenge, nor aided or assisted any person thus offending, so help me God.

tially limited the governor and other major state officials to serving only one four-year term. (They could, however, run for that same office again after being out of office.) But in 1992, voters passed an amendment to the constitution, allowing officials to serve two full terms in a row. If a governor resigns, is impeached, or dies during his or her term, the lieutenant governor becomes governor for the rest of that term.

Kentucky Lives: Bert Combs

Bert Combs seemed an unlikely person to be elected governor, but he became one of Kentucky's best chief executives of the twentieth century.

Combs was born in Clay County in eastern Kentucky. He went to a two-room schoolhouse and later rode a pony to get to high school. A very bright boy, he finished high school at age fifteen. Combs became a lawyer and moved to Prestonsburg in Floyd County. He served in World War II and returned home to Kentucky.

Quiet and not a particularly good public speaker, Combs seemed better suited to be a judge than a politician. In fact, he served six years as a justice on Kentucky's highest court. Combs had to take a pay cut to accept the judgeship, but he believed that the people of his region needed someone to speak for them on the court. Powerful political leaders wanted him to ▶

apply his talents to other offices and convinced him to run for governor in 1955, but he lost.

Four years later, Combs ran for governor again and won. At the same time the voters elected him governor, they also approved a sales tax to pay bonus money to those who had served in the armed forces and to pay for other things the state needed. With those funds, Governor Combs helped expand schools, human services, roads, and much more. To try to keep politics out of state government, he set up a merit system so that workers would not have to worry about losing their jobs each time a new governor came to Frankfort.

After Combs left office, he led the legal team that pushed for changes in education. His work helped bring about the Kentucky Education Reform Act. He died in 1991, when his car was caught in a flash flood near his home in Powell County.

Combs once said: "I think all of us would like to leave a few tracks around to let people know we've been here." Kentucky honored him by naming the Bert T. Combs Mountain Parkway for him, but he left tracks much wider than that. People knew that Bert Combs had been here.

The Judicial Branch

The judicial branch is located on the second floor of the capitol. Like the other branches of government, the courts operate on three levels. Courts on the local and state levels were set up by an amendment to the state constitution in 1975. District and circuit courts hear cases at the local level, and decisions are made by either a judge or a jury.

Parties involved in a case may appeal the decision. At the state level,

Kentucky Voices

In 1985, some citizens who considered Kentucky's educational system unfair asked the court to determine whether Kentucky was meeting its constitutional requirements in that regard. A circuit court judge found that the system, in fact, did not do as the constitution required and ruled that the state had to come up with a more equitable system of funding its schools. On appeal to the Kentucky Supreme Court, *Rose v. Council for Better Schools* (1989) became a pathbreaking case. The Supreme Court went beyond the circuit court's ruling and concluded that Kentucky's existing ▶

school system was actually unconstitutional and that a new one must be created. The court said:

This decision applies to the entire sweep of the system—all its parts and parcels. . . . Since we have, by this decision, declared the system of common schools in Kentucky to be unconstitutional, Section 183 [of the constitution] places an absolute duty on the General Assembly to re-create, re-establish a new system. We view this decision as an opportunity for the General Assembly to launch the Commonwealth into a new era of educational opportunity which will ensure a strong economic, cultural, and political future.

In the next session of the General Assembly (1990), House Bill 940 was passed, and the governor signed it into law. As the court required, it set up a new school system. That law is now called the Kentucky Education Reform Act, or KERA.

the court of appeals and the state supreme court hear appeals. The seven-person Kentucky Supreme Court hears most of the key cases on state law. For almost 200 years, only men served as justices. The face of the court changed in the 1990s when Sara Walter Combs of Powell County became the first woman on the state supreme court, and Janet Stumbo of Floyd and Pike counties became the first woman elected to a full term as justice. Each justice is elected from a certain area of the state and serves an eight-year term.

Some cases can be appealed to the U.S. Supreme Court, with its nine justices. Supreme Court justices are selected by the president of the United States. Over the years, eleven people who were either born in Kentucky or resided there at the time have been appointed to the U.S. Supreme Court. The three most prominent justices from Kentucky were John Marshall Harlan, Louis Brandeis, and Fred Vinson. Vinson, of Louisa in eastern Kentucky, was in fact named chief justice.

Kentucky Lives: John Marshall Harlan

John Marshall Harlan became a justice of the U.S. Supreme Court when he was forty-four years old. He served in that capacity for almost thirty-four years before his death in 1911. During that time, he became known as the "Great Dissenter" because he often disagreed with the decisions made by ▸

the other justices. For instance, when the Court ruled that it was legal for a state to have separate schools for black and white students, he called that decision totally wrong. In his dissent, Harlan wrote, "Our Constitution is color-blind, and neither knows nor tolerates classes among citizens." At the time, many people did not like what he said, but he had the courage to say what he thought, and the will and the skill to say it strongly and well. Years later, a different group of justices looked at that same issue and decided that Harlan had been right; his dissenting views became the rule of law.

Harlan was born near Danville, lived in Harrodsburg, and then settled in Frankfort. In politics, he was largely a loser. Although he served as state attorney general, he ran for Congress and lost by seventy votes, and twice he was defeated in races to become governor of Kentucky. As a justice, however, he was a winner in the eyes of history. When people selected the dozen greatest Supreme Court justices of all time, they named Kentuckian John Marshall Harlan as one of them.

Kentuckian and U.S. Supreme Court Justice John Marshall Harlan. (Library of Congress Prints and Photographs Division)

Justice Vinson liked to say that he was born in jail. At the time of his birth, when most women had their children at home rather than in a hospital, his parents lived in the jail because his father was the jailer. Vinson was later elected to Congress and became friends with Harry Truman. When Truman became president, he named Vinson as chief justice. Vinson served seven years before he died in 1953 at the age of sixty-three.

The Legislative Branch

The third floor of the capitol is the home of the General Assembly, Kentucky's legislative branch. The two houses of the General Assembly are the house of representatives and the senate. To be elected a member of the house, a person must be at least twenty-four years old and must have lived in Kentucky for two years. There are 100 representatives; each serves a two-year term and may run for reelection. State senators must be at least thirty years old and must have lived in the state for six years. There are thirty-eight members of the state senate, and they are elected to four-year terms.

Until the year 2000, the legislators from both houses of the General Assembly met only every other year for a sixty-day session starting in January. In 2000, the voters approved an amendment that now allows the legislators to meet every year.

Who are these people who make the laws for the state? In a recent session, most of the 138 members of the Kentucky legislature were well-educated people. Almost 100 of the 138 had college degrees. Men outnumbered women by a count of 122 to 16; however, more women are being elected each year, as a rule. The legislators' average age was fifty-one years, and they generally belonged to either the Baptist or the Catholic Church. Many worked as attorneys, teachers, farmers, home builders or sellers, or small business owners. Many different kinds of people with many different backgrounds serve in the General Assembly.

The Mystery of "Honest Dick" Tate

"Honest Dick" Tate stole funds from the state treasury just before Kentucky wrote its fourth constitution. Because Tate had served as treasurer for twenty years, the people writing the new constitution sought to pre-

Kentucky Lives: Georgia Davis Powers

Georgia Davis Powers was the first black woman to serve in the senate of Kentucky. She was born in Springfield in Washington County in 1923. Her parents had nine children, and she was the only girl. When she was seventeen months old, a tornado destroyed her family's home, and they moved to Louisville. A dozen years later, the flood of 1937 covered their house and they had to leave it for two months. At the time, her family lived very close to where boxer Muhammad Ali grew up.

Georgia Powers attended college and then worked in an airplane factory during World War II. Later, she grew interested in working for equal rights for all races and became a close friend of Dr. Martin Luther King Jr. She was in Memphis the night he was killed.

In 1967, she won election to the senate of Kentucky and served there for more than twenty years. She focused her efforts on many projects, including an open housing law, which gave all people the same rights to buy a house.

When she wrote her memoirs, she noted at the end of the book: "I prefer just to be called an American, because that is what I am. I am more interested in how I am treated than in what I am called. I share the dream that we shall all be free!" Her book and her story are part of history. As Mae Street Kidd, another black member of the General Assembly, said: "I have always loved history. It helps you find out who you are and how you got to be who you are." Kidd and Powers knew who they were.

vent elected officials from staying in office for so long. As a result, they instituted a one-term rule that lasted for 100 years. Times change, however, and voters in 1992 finally decided to let officials serve two consecutive terms.

What happened to "Honest Dick" Tate? That remains unknown. He left behind a wife and child and kept in touch with them for a while. His letters came from Canada, Asia, and South America—then the letters stopped. Did he die? Did someone kill him for his stolen money? Did he sneak back into America? No one knows. It remains a mystery.

Known as the Old Capitol, this beautiful building served as Kentucky's capitol for some eighty years. (Courtesy of the Kentucky Historical Society)

CHAPTER FIVE

Living in Kentucky

Over the years, Kentuckians have lived and worked in many different ways. Because the state has numerous regional variations and diverse peoples, not all places have had the same characteristics at the same time. Fifty years ago, the lives of people in some parts of the state differed little from those of people living at the time of statehood, back in the late eighteenth century. In contrast, people in other parts of the commonwealth may have been living closer to the ways of the present. How, then, did the average person live? Perhaps the best way to determine that is to look at a day in the life of a person soon after Kentucky became a state and compare it to a modern-day life.

Daily Life

Today, an electric alarm clock probably wakes you up in the morning. But as late as the 1940s, almost everyone living on farms in Kentucky still had no electricity—no electric lights or radios or televisions—and no telephones. When one man saw someone talking on the newly invented telephone for the first time, he said, "Look—that old fool is talking to the wall." A century after statehood, many people rode on trains, but cars and airplanes were just beginning to be invented. Today, you can get in a car and go twenty miles in just a few minutes. For those of the past, it might have taken all day to go that far.

Once the alarm clock wakes you up, you get out of bed. On cold days, your home is probably warm; on hot days, it may be cooled by air-conditioning or an electric fan. In the past, a fireplace might offer the only warmth, and even then, it could get very cold overnight—cold enough for a glass of water to freeze. So, one of the first things people did in the morning was to start a fire. Until the twentieth century, matches were not common in homes. A boy from the Jackson Purchase area recalled that if the fire in his house went out, he had to walk a mile to the next house to bring fire back from a neighbor. A century ago, a woman from Owsley County in eastern Kentucky recalled that "it was a common thing for people to go to their neighbors to borrow fire."

Beds of the past were different from those of today. You probably sleep on a mattress, covered with sheets and blankets, supported by a set of springs underneath. In frontier times, the mattress might be filled with straw and be placed on either ropes or wood planks for support. Other beds were filled with feathers. Sleepers would sink deep into those feather beds, which would help keep them warm in winter (but have the opposite effect in summer). Each year, people would refill their mattresses with fresh straw or new feathers. They often slept under heavy quilts during cold weather, since their hand-built houses might have cracks in the walls. In the twentieth century, one Barren County man in south-central Kentucky said, "In the winter when the snow blew it often came through the cracks and [got] on our beds." Some of those hand-made quilts still survive, revealing interesting patterns and histories.

Today, indoor plumbing and bathrooms are the rule. A century ago, a family might have had a "slop jar" or a bowl that they used for a toilet, after they awoke. They would then throw the contents out into the yard. Most people used an outside privy or an outhouse. Other people simply went into the woods. Either way, cold and rain could make it an unpleasant experience.

In this "Graveyard Quilt," little coffins are sewn around the border. When a person died, his or her name would be sewn onto one of these coffins, which would then be moved to the "graveyard" in the center. (Courtesy of the Kentucky Historical Society)

One of the things we take for granted is electricity—the ability to flip a switch to turn on a light. Louisville had the first electric lights in the state, installed in the 1870s. So people either got up in the dark or rose when the sun did. Their days might last from dawn to sundown, but no later. Some people had lamps that burned whale oil or coal oil to produce a faint light, but the lamps had to be cleaned often because of the soot that accumulated in the lampshade.

You might take a shower in the morning, but people of the past generally had no running water. They had to make do with a pitcher of water and a washbowl on a stand, with water obtained from a well or even a nearby stream. If they had soap, it was homemade. People took fireplace ashes, ran water over them, boiled that mixture, and then added hog or even bear fat until soap formed and could be scooped off the bottom. Kentuckians made soap that way well into the twentieth century.

Clothes and Fashion

Over the years, fashion, clothing, and appearances have changed drastically and sometimes rapidly. For instance, men of Daniel Boone's time wore their hair long; later, most men cut their hair shorter; then, in the 1960s, some men let their hair grow long again. During the time of Abraham Lincoln, men tended to wear beards. A century later, only a few men had beards. Currently, a mix of hairstyles and beards exists.

Women's fashions have changed as well. A century ago, people thought it scandalous for a woman to show any part of her leg above the ankle in public. Sixty years later, women were wearing miniskirts. Shoe styles have also changed from time to time.

In earlier times, the clothing of the average person who worked on a farm did not change as much as that of the average urbanite. At first, people made most clothes themselves, a time-consuming process. If they wanted to add color, they usually had to make their own dye from tree bark. Later, people could buy more things at nearby stores, and still later, they purchased clothes from mail-order catalogs—just as people shop over the Internet today. The invention of the sewing machine also helped people make better clothes.

Almost all children and many adults wore no shoes at certain times of the year. A man born in 1800 wrote, "All the children, both male and female, went barefoot from early spring until late in the fall." A hundred years later, a Danville boy noted that he had never worn shoes until he was five years old. If people did wear shoes, they did not have to worry about whether they had the shoe on the correct foot. They simply bought two shoes and wore them to make them fit a certain foot. Not until well after the middle of the nineteenth century did most shoes have a right and a left foot.

People dressed simply. In warm weather, usually only wealthy people wore any underclothing. In colder weather, both rich and poor people might put on flannel "long johns." When they worked in the fields, men tended to wear overalls or jeans, while women wore loose dresses.

Women in the nineteenth century tried to protect their skin from the sun as much as possible. They wore long sleeves, long dresses, bonnets, and hats, or they carried umbrellas to keep the sun off their faces. That practice changed in the twentieth century, when getting a suntan became popular for both men and women. Well into the twentieth century, people had no zippers in their clothes and used buttons instead.

When people "dressed up"—usually to go to church—they put on different clothes. Men wore wool suits and vests in both winter and summer, with heavily starched shirt collars and cuffs. Sitting in a hot building in such clothes could be very uncomfortable. Early in the nineteenth century, women wore large, heavy "hoop" skirts that made movement difficult, and their long dresses often dragged on the ground; they also wore tight, laced corsets to make themselves appear thin. The invention of the bicycle late in that century encouraged looser clothing for women so that they could ride the new contraptions.

At the end of the day, you remove your dirty clothes and put them in the washer and dryer or take them to the dry cleaner. Until the twentieth century, however, such machines were rare. Instead, women would put the family's clothes in soapy water and use a paddle or a stick to beat the wet clothes to get the dirt out. To iron the clothes, women would heat several irons over the fireplace or on the stove, and as one iron cooled, they would replace it with a hot one.

Food

These days, people can go to a grocery store and buy everything they need to prepare a meal. Canned and frozen foods are convenient, and fresh fruit and vegetables, bread, meat, and milk fill the shelves all year long. For a change, people can eat out at a restaurant, get a fast-food meal, or bring home a variety of takeout cuisine. But things differed greatly 200 and even 100 years ago.

In their limited economic system, it was difficult to get food and supplies from far away. People usually had to supply their own food, and they did so in many ways. Most farms had gardens where people grew many of the vegetables they used—corn, green beans, potatoes, peas, peppers, and more. Hunting and fishing provided meat for the table, and many farms also had chickens. People used the eggs daily and sometimes killed the chickens for food as well. One of the key sources of meat was the hog. In the fall, when it became cool enough to keep the meat fresh, hog killing took place. People would kill a hog, scrape off all its hair, drain out all the blood, and then cut up the meat into bacon, chops, jowls, and other pieces. Some of it would be ground up, made into sausage, and stored in the hog's intestines or in cloth sacks to "season."

Since people of the past had no electric or gas refrigerators, they did several things to preserve their food. They could lower it into a well or a cold spring. In the winter, they might cut ice from a frozen pond or river

Many farm families slaughtered their own livestock for food. (Courtesy of the Kentucky Historical Society)

and put it in icehouses—small buildings, mostly underground, where the ice would last longer. By the late nineteenth century, people who lived in or near towns could also buy ice from an ice factory. Each day, households would put out signs saying how much ice they wanted— maybe fifty or sixty pounds—and the delivery wagons would bring it to their homes and place it in their iceboxes—early versions of the refrigerator.

Meat could also be salted or smoked and kept in a smokehouse. Present-day salty country ham involves the same process. One boy recalled that in his family's smokehouse his mother always had ham, deer meat, and opossum to eat. People also preserved vegetables by drying them in the sun or, later, by canning. One eastern Kentucky woman recalled that her family had "dried beans, dried pumpkin, green beans dried with the hull on, and black eyed peas. I have been hungry many times for more nourishing food. All children were."

For Kentuckians of the nineteenth and early twentieth centuries, their food choices were generally limited to what they could grow or kill. Some honey or molasses might flavor a meal, but often the food remained the same from day to day. In one region of Kentucky, a person recalled that the daily fare tended to be fat pork, beans, potatoes, cornbread, coffee, and a little honey.

Later, people had more choices when country stores opened nearby. One man recalled that in his boyhood, the nearest store and post office were ten miles away. It took him half a day to get there and back. Others lived closer to a country store, which became the economic and social center of the area. There, people might receive their mail, buy groceries, purchase things for the farm, try on clothes, and just visit with friends. Most people would buy or barter for the staples—flour, salt, sugar, and coffee—at the country store. But they also had access to many other commodities—a little of everything. Want material to make a dress? The country store could supply it. Want a new pair of shoes? You could buy them. Need a new plow for the farm? It could be bought. Want to try something new to eat? The owner could offer canned oysters or canned sardines. Need some pills for an illness? You could purchase them there. From birth to death—from baby clothes to coffins—the country store kept Kentuckians supplied with what they needed.

Most farmers did not have a lot of cash and perhaps got money only

Kentucky Voices

Henry V. Johnson grew up on a farm in Scott County, Kentucky, in the middle of the nineteenth century and remembered his life this way:

We got our ice from the creek, and in summer we would go fishing and rowing on the Elkhorn.

We had a large garden. We raised many chickens and turkeys, and always had six or eight fat hogs to make sausage and bacon and smoked hams. We had a beautiful cow [that] would bring in great buckets of rich, foamy milk.

We raised all the fruit and vegetables we needed. We put up all the potatoes, cabbage, beets, turnips, and such things for winter. Wheat and corn we sent to our miller, and [we] had all the flour and meal we needed. With the exception of coffee and tea and fancy groceries, we had all on our little farm that we needed. Those were certainly the good old days!

Were they? Perhaps, but Johnson said nothing about all the hard work on the farm. Nor did he mention the fact that slaves did much of the labor. It was not the "good old days" for them.

once a year when they sold their crops. So the country store also served as a bank. The owner sold items on credit and wrote down in a ledger the buyers' names and how much they owed. Once a year, people would pay off their debts—or go into more debt to the owner of the store. Credit existed long before credit cards did.

Work

In comparing present-day life with past life, conditions varied from city to farm as well as from one time to another. In the city, people had access to more commodities and to greater educational and social activities, such as libraries and theaters. Yet cities had some special problems too. Because people burned coal to heat their houses, "this resulted in an atmosphere laden with smoke and soot and was the bane of the housewife hanging out her laundry for drying." When snow fell, it looked like it "had been gone over with a huge pepper-shaker."

The majority of early Kentuckians lived on farms, however, and seldom went to the city. In 1850, the residents of Whitley County, in south-eastern Kentucky, had the following occupations:

961 farmers	4 millers	1 boat builder
15 blacksmiths	4 barrel makers	1 carpenter
8 preachers	3 doctors	1 grain dealer
8 merchants	2 stonecutters	1 coal miner
7 schoolteachers	2 lawyers	1 silver miner
5 store clerks	2 hat makers	1 chair maker
5 shoe and boot makers	2 tailors	1 sheriff
4 laborers	2 wagon makers	

In Whitley County, more than nine out of ten people worked on farms. The same held true in other counties in Kentucky.

In good weather, the men and young boys would usually work in the fields. Some of them liked that work. One recalled, "There is a sort of thrill that comes to a barefoot boy when he plows up the ground, turns it over, and steps into the fresh furrow with his bare feet. There is a good feel and a good smell to the earth." Others liked to see things grow. But farming was hard work. Walking behind a mule pulling a plow across the dusty ground on a warm day could be hot and tiring. Farmers planted their crops, kept the weeds out, and hoped it would rain enough—but not too much. Then they harvested their crops, kept what they needed to feed themselves and their animals, and used what was left (if any) to pay off debts. Winter might bring relief from tending crops, but not from tending the cows, chickens, goats, sheep, mules, horses, and other animals. Someone had to get up early to take care of the farm animals every day of the year.

Women worked just as hard as men on the farm. A woman spent her days doing a lot of different things. She helped on the farm by tending the garden, milking the cows, and gathering the eggs. In her home, she cooked three meals a day and cleaned the dishes. She washed and ironed clothes, swept the floors, dusted, sewed new clothes and mended old ones, and made quilts. She might churn and make butter, peel apples, or can food. She also had to take care of her children, and people usu-ally had big families. Often the children would help out with some of the chores. Despite all this work, a woman's life could be very lonely. If she lived far from neighbors or the local church, a woman might not see

---

Kentucky Voices

Below are accounts of daily life by two women from Louisville. One wrote her story in 1837, and the other described her life 110 years later, in 1947. Can you tell which is which?

Account A

[My normal week:] *Monday—wash clothes and woodwork. Tuesday—iron, finish woodwork, darn socks. Wednesday—bake, garden, mend clothes. Thursday—catch up. Friday—clean house and wax floors. Saturday—perhaps bake and Bill's home, so working with him washing walls or fixing lawn. Sunday—church and relax.*

Account B

I should like to tell how I spend the day. I rise at 6:00 and start a fire with shavings and cord wood. We drink coffee at half-past six and eat meat and wheat bread with butter. I dress the children, fix the beds and straighten up the rooms. This takes most of the morning. We eat our main meal. After the dishes are washed, I clean up again. When this is done, I have to sew, patch, or knit until towards evening. I prepare coffee or tea which are taken together with bread, butter, meat, and fried potatoes.

Account A is the 1947 description. One hint is the mention of yard work—not a common, everyday practice in 1837—as well as the husband's presence at home on Saturday. Most people worked Saturdays in earlier times.

---

anyone but her husband and children for months at a time. The men often went on hunting and fishing trips with other men or rode to town or to the country store, so they had more variety in their lives.

Something that made a woman's job even harder was the ever-present dust. Even in towns and cities, most roads were not paved, and as people and horses traveled the dirt roads, clouds of dust arose. People had to leave their windows open to let in fresh air, and few homes had window screens until the twentieth century. This made it almost impossible to keep the dust out of the house, even for the hardest-working housewife. The open windows also let in flies and other insects.

Yet, many adults remembered the fun they had growing up on the farm. They could roam and explore the surrounding woods—like a

Kentucky Lives: Linda Scott DeRosier

She was born Linda Sue Preston in a feather bed in a log house on Greasy Creek in Johnson County, Kentucky, in 1941. Her father worked in a coal mine, and her mother taught school before she got married. The family lived near where singer Loretta Lynn grew up in eastern Kentucky.

Linda's book *Creeker* tells her story. When she was young, she never thought about being anything other than a wife and a mother and living on that creek. "We saw the same folks day after day," she writes; in fact, Linda saw no strangers until she was about twelve years old. She might go to church or listen to the Grand Ole Opry and the University of Kentucky Wildcats on the radio, but that was all. It was hard, she writes, "for us to find heroes; God and the Wildcats had to do." She had a small worldview.

She tells of those days in the 1950s: "My typical morning involved getting out of bed; hauling the slop jar . . . to the toilet; cleaning myself up (taking a sponge bath) . . . ; going across the road and drawing . . . two buckets of fresh water; and carrying them back to my house; . . . eating a breakfast of sausage, eggs, biscuit, and sawmill gravy . . . ; and walking . . . to the store to . . . wait for the school bus." She eventually went on to college, married at age nineteen, had a child, then later divorced. She never grew lonely, though: "If there is a book at hand, I am never alone."

Slowly she began to see that she could do more than she had thought: "Education changes the inside of our heads so that we do not see the same world we previously saw. I read those books and truly fell in love. . . . I fell in love with ideas." Linda went on to get a PhD, taught college herself, and later married a college president. Now, as Dr. DeRosier, she still teaches and still remembers her Appalachian and Kentucky roots.

huge playground. Their parents taught them what they would need to know as adults. Young boys learned to shoot and hunt and fish; young girls learned to sew and cook at an early age. They did not expect to have many choices about what they would do when they grew up.

Health

Those open windows and flies and those barefoot walks had an effect on people's health. So did a lot of other things. Overall, people of the past lived much shorter lives than we do today. A century ago, the average American lived to be forty-seven years old. But in frontier times, people died even younger than that. Many young children died as well. In some Kentucky counties, one-third of newborn babies never reached their first birthday.

Some of the diseases that struck so hard back then have little or no effect on today's Kentuckians. Smallpox, cholera, tuberculosis, polio, and deadly flu epidemics killed thousands of men, women, and children of all ages and races. When cholera swept across Kentucky in the nineteenth century, it left whole towns almost deserted as the inhabitants either fled or died. The great Spanish flu epidemic of 1918 killed more Kentuckians than had died in World War I. In Louisville alone, the Spanish flu killed some 2,400 people. Overall, 14,000 died in Kentucky.

Many things increased the chances of getting a disease. In schools and public places, everyone drank from the same dipper at the well, a practice that spread disease easily. The many outhouses and the waste left by horses and other animals on the streets all brought flies, which spread disease. In many towns and cities that had water lines, the river water

People at Camp Taylor in Louisville wore masks to protect themselves during the 1918 flu epidemic. (Courtesy of the University of Louisville Special Collections Rare Books and Photographic Archives)

was not filtered. One person in Louisville recalled drinking the yellow, muddy water from the river every day, and it probably carried disease. In 1909 the city finally began to filter its water.

Walking barefoot also caused health problems. One study in 1913 showed that 42 percent of people in Kentucky likely had hookworms, which sapped their strength. Also, when people needed to go to a hospital, they might not be able to reach one in time. A woman who grew up in Burnside, in Pulaski County, recalled that the nearest hospital was ninety miles away. In the era of horses and wagons, that represented a very long trip.

Doctors did make house calls, however. They would get on their horses in all kinds of weather to visit the sick. Many of these doctors were excellent, caring people, but there were few requirements, so virtually anyone could call himself a doctor. Some doctors had received such poor training that people might be better off without them. One Gallatin County man recalled of his youth: "For fever, the first thing, the doctor would bleed the patient. Women would get bled for a headache. My left arm has today many scars left by the lancet." This loss of blood would often hurt the patient rather than help. Nor were there any laws limiting drug use until the twentieth century. As a result, many people took drugs that are now illegal. Unaware of the dangers, some became addicts, so the drug problem is nothing new.

Today, many of the health problems of the past have ended. Although new viruses or epidemics can still occur, causing sickness or death, the discovery of new medicines and the use of vaccinations to prevent disease have helped a great deal. Research and better-informed doctors have also aided in making Kentucky a much healthier place. These days, people live to an average age of seventy-seven—thirty years longer than a century ago. That has been one of the greatest changes over the past century. People now live almost another lifetime.

Many people from Kentucky have helped make a longer life possible. One was Dr. Ephraim McDowell, who lived and worked in a house that still stands in Danville. He first came to Kentucky over the Wilderness Road when he was twelve years old, but he later went back over the mountains and crossed the Atlantic Ocean to study medicine in Europe. He returned and became known for his skills as a doctor. Future president James K. Polk traveled all the way from Tennessee to be treated by him, for example.

Kentucky Lives: Estate Inventories

When people died in the past, an inventory was made of what they left behind. The following inventories for two people who died in Metcalfe County in south-central Kentucky in 1901 differ considerably.

Estate of David Wade

1 tea kettle	$.25	8 tumblers	$.25
1 muffin pan	$.15	1 molasses jug	$.10
1 bureau	$1.50	3 dishes	$.30
1 sugar chest	$1.00	4 pitchers	$.30
1 bookcase	$.50	2 mirrors	$.30
1 dresser	$.25	2 lamps	$.50
1 cross-cut saw	$.10	16 books	$1.05
1 blanket	$.50	2 chests	$1.75
1 mowing blade	$.25	2 bedsteads	$3.00
1 posthole digger	$.60	2 sugar bowls	$.10
1 family Bible	$1.00	12 plates	$.60
1 fruit dish	$.25	2 water buckets	$.10
7 oz. yarn	$.35	1 bushel salt	$.25
11 quilts	$6.35	6 chairs	$.75
3 tablecloths	$1.00	3 feather beds	$12.00
1 kettle	$.75	1 set knives and forks	$.50
6 curtains	$.40	1 candle stand	$.65
1 clock	$.50	2 watches	$.85

Total value: $39.05

Estate of C. C. Smith

1 mule	$65.00	25 barrels corn	$75.00
1 mare	$60.00	100 pounds bacon	$12.50
1 cow	$20.00	64 pounds lard	$8.00
1 cow	$20.00	10 barrels corn	$30.00
1 plow	$2.00	1,500 pounds millet	$6.00
1 plow harness	$1.00	47 "shoots" [pigs]	$38.50
1 hoe, 1 ax	$.25	25 shocks fodder	$1.50
1 wagon	$25.00	½ bushel salt	$.75
2 beds	$30.00	4 irons	$.40
1 table	$.50	1 churn	$.10
1 cooking stove	$3.00	1 fly brush	$.05
1 set knives and forks	$.50	1 mirror	$.40
1 set cups, saucers	$.30	1 bedstead	$1.50
1 set chairs	$5.00	1 clock	$.50
1 sewing machine	$3.00	1 surrey [wagon]	$15.00
2 beds	$6.00	1 cultivator	$8.00
1 bedstead	$3.50	1 posthole digger	$.25
1 lamp	$.40	1 washing machine	$3.50
1 dresser	$3.50	1 spade	$.60
1 wardrobe	$4.00	1 pair scales	$.10
1 washstand	$1.50	1 grindstone	$.50
1 dresser	$3.00	1 wash kettle	$1.25
1 cupboard	$2.00	1 roller	$.25
stoneware	$2.00		

Total value: $466.10

In 1809, Dr. McDowell faced a hard choice. Forty-seven-year-old Jane Todd Crawford had been diagnosed as being pregnant with twins, but McDowell correctly discovered that she actually had a deadly tumor that would kill her. Other doctors indicated that operating would result in death for the patient, but Dr. McDowell and Mrs. Crawford decided to risk it. There was no way to put her to sleep during the operation, so she sang and held on tight to the operating table. The operation went well, proving that a person's body could be opened up and that he or she could live through it. Five days after the operation, Mrs. Crawford was on her feet. Less than a month later, she rode home to Green County, where she lived to be seventy-eight years old. Dr. McDowell went on to perform the operation on other patients. He became a leader in the field of medicine, and today his statue is one of five that stands in Kentucky's capitol rotunda.

Another national leader in health care was Mary Breckinridge. Having seen both her children die young, Breckinridge wanted to spare other mothers that grief. Eastern Kentucky had few doctors, so in 1925, she went to live near Hyden in Leslie County and set up the Frontier Nursing Service. At that time, most births took place with a midwife's help. With that fact in mind, Breckinridge began to ask trained nurses to become nurse-midwives, and she set up a school to train new people as well. Over the years, she succeeded in reducing the deaths of mothers and babies in childbirth to almost zero. People from all over the world came to see what she had done.

Many other Kentuckians helped improve health care in the state. Linda Neville of Lexington started a group to help prevent trachoma, an eye disease that can cause blindness. One study found that among 4,000 people in one part of the state, almost 500 of them—one in eight—had the disease. Neville helped eliminate trachoma. Dr. Joseph N. McCormack and his son Dr. Arthur McCormack, who lived in Bowling Green, together set up county health departments to help control disease. In more recent times, doctors in Kentucky have taken a leading role in such innovations as hand and heart transplants.

Fun and Games

People worked hard and often played hard in the state's early years, but in frontier times, the division between work and play was often blurred.

The things people did for fun usually involved the family or centered on work. For example, people might come together to help build a house or to take the "shucks" off corn. When they did, they often made a game of it, with one side trying to outdo the other. Prizes might go to the winner, and at the end, they would have a party. For a long time, individuals worked this way. A century ago, an eastern Kentucky man recalled how they still worked in groups: "Most of the time we did our work as a family unit, but sometimes the neighbors were called in to help out at clearings, brush-burnings, bean-stringings, and apple-peelings, haymaking, hog-killing, and such." Entertainment included square dancing, card playing (Rook), and folk singing.

Across Kentucky, people did simple things for fun. At the end of a workday, they might simply sit on the porch, tell stories about the past, or share ghost stories. Other times, the family might sit around a flickering fire and sing folk songs, which often originated from Europe or elsewhere. Hunting and fishing helped supply food for the table, but they could also provide enjoyment for those who took part. Every now and then, in later times, something special might happen, such as a fair or a traveling circus coming through the area, bringing some excitement.

In towns and cities, more opportunities for entertainment usually existed. From almost the earliest days, Lexington had a library, a place to play billiards, and taverns where people could meet. In 1814, one visitor wrote, "Society is polished . . . and the dresses at the parties are . . . tasty and elegant." A boy of a century ago remembered that his family and friends went to watch a live play at a theater in Louisville and enjoyed picnics in the city's park system. Girls played cards, while boys went to ball games.

In frontier times, just about the only organized sport was horse racing, which has been part of Kentucky culture from the early settlement period. William Whitley of Lincoln County built a track near his home, but because he did not like the British (America's enemy in the Revolutionary War), he had horses run in the opposite direction from British tracks. That is now the American way.

Kentucky had racing all over the state. A year after statehood, Lexington passed a law against "jockeys racing their horses through the streets." By 1800, Kentucky had more horses per person than any other state, and the commonwealth quickly became known for its racehorses. The Kentucky Derby in Louisville started in 1875 and added to that fame. In

Kentucky Lives: Isaac Murphy

Many people consider Isaac Murphy the greatest American jockey of the nineteenth century. He rode in 1,412 races and won 628 of them, the best winning record of any jockey before or since. Three times he won the greatest of horse races, the Kentucky Derby. Murphy was the first to win it two years in a row. Yet his success did not come easily.

"Ike" Murphy was born the same year the Civil War started. His African American father died in the army, when Murphy was young. The boy and his mother lived in Lexington, and at age fourteen he began racing horses. At that time, most jockeys were black. In fact, in fifteen of the first twenty-eight Derbys, an African American jockey rode the winning horse.

Just five feet tall, Murphy weighed about 110 pounds—a typical weight for a jockey. Although he had a hard time keeping his weight down as he got older, Murphy still won race after race. He earned a great deal of money, and he and his wife became leaders in black society.

In 1896, Murphy died at the young age of thirty-four. Over the years, his grave became covered with weeds, and no one knew its location. Murphy seemed forgotten. Someone uncovered it years later, and one of the greatest jockeys born in Kentucky now rests with one of the greatest horses—Man o' War—at the Kentucky Horse Park. This sporting pioneer finally found his home.

Jockey Isaac Murphy. (Courtesy of the Kentucky Historical Society)

the twentieth century, such great horses as Man o' War and Secretariat increased the public's interest in the sport. Racing is the oldest major organized sport in the state.

Another sport that many people watched in the early years was boxing, but it never became as popular as some of the other sports did. At first, boxers fought without gloves. Kentucky has produced three major champions in boxing. The best known of these was Muhammad Ali, perhaps the most famous Kentuckian worldwide.

Of the so-called major sports today, baseball flourished first, being played even before the Civil War. After the Civil War, professional teams formed, and paid ballplayers played in leagues. Louisville had teams—called either the Louisville Grays or the Louisville Colonels—in the major leagues through most of the late nineteenth century. One boy recalled that the city "was really a baseball-mad place," and the newspaper offices would post the scores outside for people to see. By 1900, however, Kentucky teams played only minor league ball, although many men from the state still played at the major league level. Four were named to baseball's Hall of Fame—players Earle Combs of Owsley County, Pee Wee Reese of Elkton and Louisville, and Jim Bunning of Fort Thomas, and baseball commissioner Happy Chandler of Corydon and Versailles. All across Kentucky, however, people continued to play baseball, with different towns hosting their own semiprofessional teams. Because blacks and whites could not play together until about fifty years ago, African Americans formed their own teams. The Louisville Slugger brand baseball bat became famous, and the Slugger Museum in Louisville now tells the story of its bats.

Football became the next major sport to gain Kentuckians' interest. The first football game in the state was played as early as 1880, and it soon became the chief sport at colleges. Probably the high point for Kentucky college football came in 1921, when tiny Centre College played Harvard University (unbeaten in five years) and pulled off a stunning upset, winning by a score of 6–0. That game would later be voted the greatest upset in the first seventy years of twentieth-century football. Since that time, various teams have won national titles at different levels—Eastern Kentucky University twice, and Georgetown College three times. But none of them received as much notice as that little Centre College team called the Praying Colonels.

The last of the major sports invented is first in the hearts of many

Kentucky Voices

Even sports change over the years—both the rules and the terminology. Baseball players in the 1860s followed these rules:

1. The thrower [pitcher] must attempt to throw the ball where the striker [batter] wishes it thrown.
2. The thrower must throw the ball underhanded.
3. The striker is obligated to hit well-thrown balls. . . . The umpire may call strikes or even declare a striker dead [out] if the umpire believes the striker is consistently failing to swing at well-thrown balls.
4. Foul ticks [foul balls] do not count as strikes. Foul ticks caught in flight or on their first bounce cause the striker to be dead.
5. Runners may not slide into bases.
6. Fielders must stand in the middle of their areas until the ball is hit [e.g., the second baseman must stand on second base].
7. Runners may not lead off bases.
8. Stealing bases is prohibited. [It was considered a gentlemen's game, and gentlemen do not steal.]
9. Fly balls caught in flight or on the first bounce cause the striker to be dead.
10. All handling of the ball should be done with bare hands.
11. The behind [catcher] may play at any point up to 45 feet behind home base.
12. The shortstop may play anywhere on the field.
13. The four bases are at the corners of a square 30 yards apart.
14. Use of foul or profane language, consumption of alcoholic beverages, and gambling are prohibited.

Kentuckians today. Basketball, invented in the 1890s to give people an indoor sport to play in the winter, was initially considered a game for women. The University of Kentucky had a women's team in 1902, a year before it had one for men. For thirty years, women played basketball in the state, and then women were banned from basketball tournaments until 1975. Soon after that, women's tournaments in other sports were initiated as well—softball in 1983 and soccer in 1992.

Men's basketball grew at the college level chiefly because of the success of one man. Adolph Rupp grew up in Kansas speaking German (he later learned English). He went to college and played basketball, first for the man who invented the sport and later for the first real coach of the game. When Rupp was twenty-nine, the University of Kentucky hired him as its head coach. Called the "Baron of Basketball," he served there for the next forty-two years and won more games than anyone had in the past.

Rupp hated to lose. Few of his players liked him very much, because he was so hard on them. They did like to win, though. Four times between 1948 and 1958, Rupp's team won the national title. When someone asked him the secret to winning those titles, the immodest Rupp said, "That's easy. It's good coaching." Three others who followed Rupp

Coach Adolph Rupp (center) with members of the undefeated 1953–1954 University of Kentucky basketball team and assistant coach Harry Lancaster. (Courtesy of the University of Kentucky Special Collections and Archives)

as coaches at the University of Kentucky also won titles—Joe Hall, Rick Pitino, and Tubby Smith. With those seven national titles, the University of Kentucky ranked second in major college titles won. By 2008, it also ranked first in the number of victories among college teams. Rupp and the other coaches certainly gave Kentuckians a reason to feel good about themselves.

Other schools in the state have also achieved success playing basketball. The University of Louisville under Coach Denny Crum won two national titles in the 1980s. At the small-college level, Kentucky Wesleyan in Owensboro has won eight titles, Kentucky State University three, and Georgetown College one. Although Western Kentucky University has never won a national title, it has won many games over the years and ranks high in overall victories. Its colorful coach, Ed Diddle of Adair County, first brought the Hilltoppers national attention. In his forty-two years at the school, Diddle won his league's title thirty-two times. He, Rupp, and Crum have joined many players from Kentucky in the national Basketball Hall of Fame.

In some ways, however, the real heart of Kentucky basketball beats at the high school level. Interest in the sport sparked the growth of basketball in towns both big and small, but there was no true state tournament for high schools until 1957. Before then, black and white players had separate, segregated tournaments; after 1957, players of all races competed together to determine who had the best team. Black players such as Wes Unseld could gain statewide respect for their play, as had white players such as "King" Kelly Coleman before them. Only later would females have a tournament.

Kentucky's state high school basketball tournament, called the "Sweet 16," brings together sixteen teams from both large and small schools from all over the state. Interest in the tournament grew because of one championship game in 1928, when big-school Ashland played Carr Creek, from the mountains. Carr Creek's high school had only eight male students; the school had no gym, and the players had no uniforms. Their basketball court was outside, with a hill behind it, so if someone made a bad pass or missed a shot, the ball would roll down the hill. Those two schools played each other into four overtime periods before Ashland finally won the game. Carr Creek had won the support of Kentucky, however, even though its team had lost. Since then, people like to cheer the underdog small-school teams, such as the one from Brewers in

Marshall County, which won the 1948 title. Brewers continues to be the last undefeated team in Kentucky high school basketball history.

Kentuckians have long been interested in many sports other than the major ones. A century ago, tennis and croquet proved popular. People also joined bicycle clubs to enjoy that new invention. Now they might play golf. (One of the first golf courses in the nation was built at Middlesboro more than a century ago.) Fans watch automobile races, where several Kentuckians have been successful. In recent years, more people have begun to play soccer. Many people from Kentucky like to play different sports, and they enjoy watching them even more—another way that present-day life differs from that of a century or two ago.

Religion

Although religion constitutes an important part of many people's lives today, it formed an even more central part of individual existence in the past. Religion came to Kentucky early. Of course, the Indians had had their own religious beliefs and rituals for thousands of years. In the first year of English settlement, the settlers brought their own religious beliefs to Kentucky. Public worship first took place at Boonesborough when an Anglican minister offered a prayer. Because Kentucky was still part of England at the time, he asked for the king's blessing as well.

Soon people from many different churches arrived to settle the new land. In 1781, some 600 Baptists of the "Traveling Church" came to Kentucky from Virginia. An enslaved man called "Uncle Peter" preached to the slaves who came with them. That same year, the first Baptist church was started in Kentucky at Severns Valley, near Elizabethtown. Perhaps as many as one-fourth of all the Baptists in Virginia came to Kentucky in search of freedom to worship. Other Protestant groups came also. Bishop Francis Asbury helped start many Methodist churches, for example.

Four years after the "Traveling Church" arrived, a large number of Catholics moved from Maryland. They journeyed down the river to Maysville, then overland to Nelson County and surrounding places. As a result, those areas had a large Catholic population. The first Catholic church was established in the year of statehood, and the first Catholic priest ordained in the United States, Stephen T. Badin, came to Kentucky to help other Catholics. Bardstown became one of the first four centers for Catholics in the nation and the first one west of the mountains.

Other religious groups came later. Those of the Jewish faith, for example, set up their first place of worship fifty years after statehood and seemed to be well accepted. Somerset's first mayor was Jewish, as were an early mayor of Paducah and a later mayor of Louisville.

But the central religious event in early Kentucky was what became known as the Great Revival. Soon after statehood, a strong spirit of religious feeling started to sweep the commonwealth. It began in Logan County in western Kentucky at the Gaspar River, Red River, Muddy River, and other places. One person wrote of the worshippers: "Many fell to the ground, lay powerless, groaning, praying, and crying for mercy." The movement spread, and the biggest meeting took place in 1801 at Cane Ridge in Bourbon County, around a church that still stands. Later writers called Cane Ridge the "most important religious gathering in American history." Perhaps some 20,000 people attended the outdoor camp meeting, a number that represented almost 10 percent of Kentucky's population at the time. The Cane Ridge meeting became like a temporary city. One man said, "For more than a half mile, I could see people on their knees before God in humble prayer." Another said that you could hear the camp meeting before you could see it: "The noise was like the roar of Niagara." He wrote about "the vast sea of human beings" he found there—young and old, black and white, male and female. People who had not seen many other faces on the frontier now saw thousands. They lived during a time of great change, when life was short and danger was all around. At Cane Ridge, they could escape from everyday cares and be a part of something that seemed bigger than themselves.

Numerous changes grew out of the Great Revival. New churches sprang up, and membership in older churches increased. People had a greater sense of order in their lives after the frontier period. Churches seemed more open to new people. In Kentucky, the Disciples of Christ, or Christian Church, started and then spread throughout America. Small religious groups found a friendly home in the state as well. The best known of these was the Shakers—so called because of their dancing and shaking during worship services.

The Shakers never had many members, but they received a lot of attention because of their beliefs. They claimed that people could achieve a perfect and sinless society on earth if they would break free of the greed of the world and live pure lives. Establishing villages at Pleasant Hill in central Kentucky and at South Union in the more western part of the state, the Shakers tried to live out their beliefs. No member could own property, and men and women had to stay apart in all ways. For Shakers, a typical day consisted of the following: arise at four in the morning, work for an hour and a half, eat breakfast (men and women sitting silently at separate tables), more work, lunch, work again, supper at six, prayers, and then to bed. The last Kentucky Shaker died in 1923, but the beautiful Shaker villages still remind us of their ideals.

While the Shakers were gaining members, black churches also developed. The oldest may have been the First African Baptist Church in Lexington, started by a slave named Peter who was known as "Old Captain." He may have been the first black preacher in the state. London Ferrill, a freed slave, followed him as church leader. By the time of Ferrill's death before the Civil War, that church had more than 1,800 members, making it the largest church in Kentucky. The Reverend George Dupee set up many other African American churches across the state, especially in western Kentucky. Religion was important to African Americans, and churches helped them develop leaders who would guide the black community once slavery ended and freedom came. These houses of worship also gave enslaved people places to come together where they could talk and hope. Churches offered them the promise of a better life in the future.

At many white churches at the time, women sat on one side of the church and men on the other during worship services. Most buildings had little or no heat, so in winter, people warmed bricks in the fire, wrapped the bricks in cloth, and brought them to church to keep their feet warm. A service usually lasted from two to three hours. Some churches had music, but others considered it sinful. After the preaching, the parishioners might have a meal on the church grounds, weather permitting. This gave them a chance to talk to their neighbors, and young people often met their future spouses that way. Going to church became both a religious and a social event.

Less than a century ago, a group of churches said that dancing was "indecent, immoral, and immodest." They called movies "the devil's workshop." That same group also attacked card playing, Sunday baseball games, and horse racing. Other churches considered these practices acceptable. Such differences continue to exist among religions.

Today, half of all church members in Kentucky belong to the Baptist Church. The next largest religious groups are the Catholics and the

Kentucky Lives: Thomas Merton

Thomas Merton was born in France to a New Zealander father and an American mother. By age fifteen, he was orphaned. After college, he joined a group of Catholic monks in Trappist, Kentucky, near Bardstown. He became a U.S. citizen and lived in Kentucky the rest of his life.

The monks worshipped as simply as possible. Their clothes, their life of prayer, and their hard work did not differ much from those of people living centuries earlier. First of all, they almost never spoke, using sign language instead. On a typical day, Merton and the other monks would wake at two o'clock in the morning, go to prayers, and then read until dawn. For breakfast, they did not eat meat, eggs, or cheese; in fact, they ate as little food as they could. At seven o'clock in the evening, they went to bed. The monks slept fully clothed on straw mattresses with wood frames. They had little heat, and water sometimes froze in the rooms where they slept. They felt that this hard life helped make their spirits strong.

Merton stood out because he wrote. He was not allowed to do so for more than two hours a day, but that was enough time. His book *The Seven Storey Mountain* told the saga of his life to that point and became an international best seller. That and his other religious writings made him world famous. He was critical of wealth, while there were still poor people in the world. He wrote against war when there could be peace. He opposed waste when there could be plenty.

In 1968, at age fifty-three, Merton finally got to travel to other nations to study and learn from their religions. While in Thailand for a Buddhist-Christian meeting, Merton stepped from his hotel shower, touched an electric fan, and was electrocuted. He died exactly twenty-seven years to the day after becoming a monk. Thomas Merton is Kentucky's best-known religious figure.

Methodists. The Presbyterians have their national headquarters in Louisville, a symbol that, as in the past, religion is important to many Kentucky citizens.

Although there are many differences between the way people live now and the way they lived in the past, the people of each period share some very basic things. All people go through the same cycle—birth, life, death. In all ages, people fall in love and have children. They share the same fears and the same hopes for a better future. They know happiness and sorrow. They have victories and defeats. No matter what the time period, people share common emotions and are bonded to their fellow humans of earlier times. They all form part of Kentucky's continuing story.

Large outdoor meetings like this one brought thousands of people together in the Great Revival of 1801. (Courtesy of the Kentucky Historical Society)

CHAPTER SIX

From Statehood to the Civil War

Between Kentucky's statehood in 1792 and the start of the Civil War in 1861, the commonwealth grew rapidly. On the surface, visitors found the state a good place to live. They noted the many inventions, the good college in Lexington, the strong business growth of Louisville, the rich farms of western Kentucky, and more. By the middle of that period, people visited the state and wrote of what they found.

One man called Lexington "a lively handsome city. The streets are all lined with shade trees. There is much show and luxury here." Another said that Louisville's Main Street "presents a proud display of wealth. . . . The present inhabitants are the most hospitable in the Western States." A third traveler referred to Bowling Green as "a thriving and handsome town" with a good future. He noted that "the very beautiful" city of Hopkinsville had a "society uncommonly friendly," and he found Henderson's citizens "intelligent, frank, and hospitable."

One visitor wrote that in Kentucky, "every man stands on his own individual merits." But that was not true. Behind the nice towns and the friendly people that these visitors described, there was another Kentucky that refused to let a large number of people in the state stand on their own merits and abilities—the enslaved. The visitors said little or nothing about the slaves, even though much of Kentucky's wealth came from slave labor. Slaves' lives were part of the hidden story of the state.

Slavery

Long before the English began to settle in Kentucky, slavery existed in America. During the trip from Africa across the ocean to the New World, many slaves died. Once the survivors arrived in North America, they had to adopt a new language and a new religion. They had to learn about new crops and new ways of doing things. They kept some of their old ways, however, such as singing African songs and retaining some African words, which are now part of the English language. The culture that the slaves developed was not truly African, nor was it fully European, for each group changed the other. It was American.

Slavery had been in America for more than 150 years when Kentucky was first settled. People from Virginia and other places brought slaves with them into the new area. Early explorer Christopher Gist had only his black slave with him when he traveled to Kentucky in the 1750s. Daniel Boone turned back after his first trip to settle the land, but slaves had been part of that group. On his next try, a slave and a white man died in an Indian attack. The two men were buried side by side; the survivors considered them equal in death, even if they did not treat them as equal in life. A slave later died defending Boonesborough. One out of ten people in early Fort Harrod was a slave. Blacks and whites fought together, and both shaped Kentucky.

When Kentuckians met to write a constitution in 1792, they voted on whether to keep slavery or end it. They kept it by a vote of twenty-six to sixteen. Those twenty-six had seemingly forgotten that blacks and whites had fought as equals against their shared enemy. They did not consider that both groups had worked to build a state out of the wilderness. They could not throw off their old ways totally, even on this new frontier. So they planned for their freedom as a new state, but they excluded slaves from that freedom, and slavery continued.

A visitor wrote: "The fertility of the lands generally vastly exceed any thing I ever saw before. But, O Alas! Here, as in Virginia, the slavery of the human race is unfortunately tolerated. Here the cries of the oppressed are heard." Those cries would go on for a long time.

At the time of statehood, about one-quarter of the white families in the new state owned at least one slave. The average number of slaves per family was 4.3. About a half century later, more families had slaves, and the average number had gone up to 5.4 slaves per family. One man in Henderson owned 214 human beings. Although well over half the white families in Kentucky did not own slaves, many of them still supported the slave system. Slavery was not about to end on its own in Kentucky.

Slave Life

Many people have tried to compare slavery to some situation in modern life. Some have likened it to being a private in the army: you have to obey orders and do what people say, but you have some free time to yourself.

Kentucky Lives: Slaves versus Free

The table below shows the percentage of slaves in Kentucky before the Civil War.

Year	% Free	% Slaves
1790	84	16
1800	82	18
1810	80	20
1820	78	22
1830	76	24
1840	77	23
1850	79	21
1860	80	20

Here are some more numbers from 1850 for the states that allowed slavery.

State	Number of Slaveholders	Average Number of Slaves per Family
Alabama	29,295	11.7
Arkansas	5,999	7.8
Delaware	809	2.8
Florida	3,520	11.2
Georgia	38,456	9.9
Kentucky	38,385	5.5
Louisiana	20,670	11.8
Maryland	16,040	5.6
Mississippi	23,116	13.4
Missouri	19,185	4.6
North Carolina	28,303	10.2
South Carolina	25,596	15.0
Tennessee	33,864	7.1
Texas	7,747	7.5
Virginia	55,063	8.6

Others have compared life as a slave to being in jail: there might be some time when you can do what you want, but you are limited by the walls around you and the guards watching over you. Of course, the main difference is that you can be discharged from the army, and a prison term can end. Slavery was for life. Those in the system were born into it and died under it.

Many people (both black and white) who observed slavery in Kentucky pronounced it less harsh in Kentucky than in other slave states.

This rare drawing shows slaves working in the hemp fields. The owner's home can be seen in the background, with slave dwellings around it. (Courtesy of the Kentucky Historical Society)

But, in a sense, whether that is true or not really does not matter. Slavery was still slavery, a system in which one person controlled another. If given the choice of being well fed and warm in prison or being hungry and cold but free, almost all slaves would have picked freedom. One wrote: "Better liberty with poverty, than plenty with slavery." But freedom remained a distant dream for most slaves.

How people treated slaves differed from one place to another. Some masters might treat slaves as well as could be expected under the system. Others might abuse them badly. Some owners might provide food and clothes similar to those given to free workers. Others might give slaves very little. In such ways, slavery differed everywhere, from place to place, and from person to person.

One thing, however, was the same: the buying and selling of human beings revealed a cruel, harsh system. People would read newspaper ads like this one from Bardstown in 1809: "For sale a negro man and woman, each about twenty-four years of age, both are excellent plantation hands, together with two children. They will be sold separately or

Kentucky Voices

In 1840, slave owner John Young of Laurel County in eastern Kentucky wrote his will. When he died seven years later, it went into effect. Here is how he disposed of his slaves:

I make the following dispositions from a principal [sic] of humanity. I therefore give and bequeath to my daughter Polly Parker my boy Slave Wiley until he arrives at the age of twenty-five years at which time he is to be free. . . . I give and bequeath my boy Slave Green to my Grandson Hiram upon the same conditions. . . . And to my daughter Theny Johnson I give and bequeath my boy Slave Deake upon the same conditions and limitations as above. . . . And to my daughter Susan Johnson I give and bequeath my girl Slave Polly until she shall be 21 years of age when she is also to be free. As to my Slave Sally it is my desire that she shall be free at my death, but as to Juliann . . . I will that she remain a Slave, and I give and bequeath her to my son Pleasant but the child she is now pregnant with I give and bequeath to my little granddaughter Theney. . . . All of the children of Juliann in future . . . shall be free at 25 years of age.

together." Some slaves sold at slave markets stayed in the state. Others were shipped farther south. Perhaps 80,000 Kentucky slaves never saw their Kentucky homes again after they went on the auction block. Even if a slave owner did not want to sell them, they could be sold after his or her death to pay off the owner's debts. Under the law, slaves were just property, just like a horse or a house.

Eleven-year-old slave Isaac Johnson and his family were put up for sale. He was sold first. His four-year-old brother Ambrose went next, sold to someone else. When Isaac's mother came before the crowd, she held baby Eddie in her arms. Someone yelled out to sell them separately. The auctioneer took the baby from her and sold him; then he sold the mother to another person. Isaac never saw any of his family again. Slavery harmed all it touched, black and white.

Those who were not sold and taken south made the best living they could under slavery. With hope for a better day, they married. Preachers usually did not ask slaves to say that they would be married "till death do us part." Slave couples vowed that the marriage would go on until ended by "death or distance"—that is, until one of them was sold. Strong black families grew, despite their problems.

In Louisville, black preacher Henry Adams of Fifth Street Baptist Church started one of the first schools for African Americans in Kentucky. All across the state, black churches sprang up. At least seventeen of those churches existed before the Civil War. There, the music of spirituals gave slaves a sense of worth and hope for a better life in the future. That enslaved people could build such full lives shows the strength of the human spirit. Some also worked to gain their freedom, unwilling to wait for some distant future when they might be free.

Freedom

A few slaves—very few—either were freed by their masters or bought their freedom. The best known were the slaves York and Frank.

The famous Lewis and Clark expedition to the Pacific Ocean and back could be said to have started in Louisville, where the two leaders first met. About half the people on that trip had some tie to Kentucky. One of them was a slave named York, owned by William Clark. Born in Virginia, York had come to Kentucky before statehood. By joining Lewis and Clark's group, he apparently became the first African American to cross the present-day United States. He became an important member of the team, for many Indians had never seen a black man and thought that York had great powers. He also hunted and aided in other ways. The men gave him full voting rights when they had to make a decision. What they found on their trip set the stage for the next wave of settlers moving west.

When the most famous exploring trip in American history ended, York remained a slave, however. When his master finally freed him in gratitude for his help on the trip, York disappeared from the historical record. Some say that he died of disease in another state. Others say that he went back to Indian lands and became a chief. Either way, he died a free man. Most people who had been born slaves could not say that.

The man who became known as Free Frank got his freedom another way. A few owners allowed their slaves to work to earn money, once they had finished the master's work for the day. Frank spent almost all his time working so that he could earn enough money to buy his freedom. Born a slave in South Carolina, Frank came with his owner to Pulaski

County, Kentucky, where he met his wife and started a family. Frank hired himself out to work, and after seven years he had enough money to buy his wife's freedom. He got her out of slavery first because, under the law, children were free or slave depending on the mother's status. Frank wanted any children they had to be born free. Two years later, he had the funds to buy his own freedom. Afterward, he kept working and used the money to purchase the freedom of others.

In 1830, members of Frank's freed family moved to Illinois, where he set up a new town. He died in 1854 at the age of seventy-seven. Frank stated in his will that some of his land should be sold to buy freedom for even more family members, and that money freed seven of his grandchildren and great-grandchildren. Overall, Frank bought the freedom of sixteen people. But not many slaves had the opportunity to do that.

The stories of York and Frank were unusual. Most masters did not free their slaves, and very few slaves had the opportunity to purchase their freedom. For most slaves who wanted to be free, escape offered the only option, but few made that dangerous choice. It was hard for a whole family to escape, and runaway slaves who were caught might be taken from their families and sold down the Ohio River out of Kentucky. Other owners whipped slaves who tried to run away. Most slaves resisted slavery in other ways. They might work very slowly or deliberately break their work tools and call it an accident.

For years, people said that runaway slaves found freedom with the aid of the Underground Railroad. That name came about when someone asked a Kentucky master how his slaves had escaped, and he said that they must have taken an underground road to safety. Of course, the Underground Railroad was neither underground nor a railroad. According to the stories, a well-planned system helped slaves escape. They would be taken or would travel on their own from one "safe" house to another. Whites and a few free blacks helped them reach safety and freedom.

Actually, in Kentucky and in most of the South, runaway slaves usually escaped to free states with little aid. It was just too dangerous to trust anyone in slave states. But once slaves reached one of the free states north of the Ohio River, they might get help from people who disliked slavery. Josiah Henson and most other African American slaves took no "railroad." They escaped on their own.

In a few cases, slaves had help from other sources, mostly from the few free blacks in Kentucky. The most famous white people to help run-

Kentucky Lives: Josiah Henson

President Abraham Lincoln said that the book *Uncle Tom's Cabin* helped lead the United States into the Civil War because it caused people to see the evils of slavery. The author of that book, Harriet Beecher Stowe, based part of what she wrote on her visits to Kentucky slaves. Though different slaves may have been the model for Uncle Tom, one model may have been Josiah Henson of Daviess County in western Kentucky.

Henson was born into slavery in the state of Maryland. His owner sent him to Owensboro, Kentucky, to work, where Henson heard both white and black preachers and became a Methodist minister. Still a slave, he tried to raise money to buy his freedom. His master cheated him, however, and Henson learned that he and his family might be sold and sent to the Deep South. In the middle of September 1830, on a dark, moonless night, Henson, his wife, and their four children got in a boat and fled across the Ohio River into a free state. By law, his owner could return Henson or any of his family to slavery if they were recaptured, so they hid in the woods during the daytime and moved only at night. They had little to eat, and the hungry and tired children cried. It took them two weeks to reach Cincinnati, where they finally got food. Then they headed farther north, making it almost to Canada despite the sharp briars that tore their clothes and the frightening howls of wild animals. A friendly white boat captain took them on the last stage of their journey—into Canada, where no slave catcher could get them. There Henson preached and started a school. Twice he returned to Kentucky to lead other slaves to freedom. Whether Stowe used him as her model for Uncle Tom is uncertain.

We do know that Kentucky's state song, written by Stephen Collins Foster, was originally called "Poor Uncle Tom, Good Night." Now, of course, its title is "My Old Kentucky Home." The words can be read as the lament of slaves who had been sold far away from their old Kentucky home.

aways were Delia Webster and Calvin Fairbank. Webster, a teacher, and Fairbank, a preacher, both came from the North to Lexington, and both hated slavery. They helped slave Lewis Hayden and his family escape, but afterward, someone found out what they had done, and the two went to jail as "slave stealers." Webster received a pardon soon after and moved to Trimble County, where she helped more slaves escape; eventually, Kentuckians forced her to leave the state. Fairbank had a harder time. He served five years in prison, but soon after his release he started helping runaways again. Imprisoned a second time, he eventually served twelve more years. During that confinement, Fairbank counted the times he was whipped: he said he received 35,105 lashes. When he finally got out of prison, his weight had dropped from 180 pounds to 117 pounds, and his friends did not recognize him. He had suffered greatly for living by his principles.

In one case near Danville, a college student gathered some slaves together and they fled as a group—some forty to seventy of them. They made it to Bracken County, within fifteen miles of the Ohio River and freedom, before pursuers caught them. The student was sent to prison and died there.

Most of those who gained freedom by running away did so alone. William Wells Brown, for example, was born in Kentucky and was later taken to Missouri, where he worked on a steamboat. When it landed on free soil one day, he got off and fled. Brown then helped others escape and wrote about his efforts in a book. Threats on his life forced him to go to Europe for five years, where he ended up writing a novel—the first known novel written by an African American.

Henry Bibb was born into slavery in Shelby County, Kentucky. After he married, his wife's owner bought him and took him to Trimble County. There, at the age of twenty-two, he escaped. When Bibb came

Henry Bibb escaped from slavery several times before he was finally freed. (Library of Congress Prints and Photographs Division)

back to try to free his wife and child, "slave catchers" seized him, but he escaped from them. After Bibb tried and failed again to free his wife, the owner sold Bibb and his family down the river to the Deep South. Once more, Bibb escaped by following the North Star to freedom in Canada. Bibb later wrote to his former owner, telling him why he had left: "To be compelled to stand by and see you whip and slash my wife without mercy when I could afford her no protection . . . was more than I felt it to be the duty of a slave husband to endure. . . . My infant child was also frequently flogged . . . until its skin was bruised literally purple."

Henry Bibb, William Wells Brown, Josiah Henson, and Lewis Hayden all became free. Their lives showed what slaves could do once they were free. But very few slaves had that chance.

Antislavery

Rather than trying to help individual slaves escape directly, some white Kentuckians wanted to end the whole system of slavery. They did not agree on how that should happen, but they did agree that slavery should stop.

At first, a few argued that slaves should be freed and sent back to Africa. However, by that time, the parents and grandparents of most slaves had been born in North America, and they considered the United States their home. They were Americans, not Africans. As a result, the movement failed, and only 661 former slaves from Kentucky went to Africa.

Others spoke out in stronger terms, saying that slavery itself should end. Some argued that it should be phased out over a period of time, while others demanded that it end immediately. The most colorful person among this group was Cassius M. Clay of White Hall in Madison County. He once said, "I believe slavery to be an evil—an evil morally, economically, physically, intellectually, socially, religiously, politically, an unmixed evil." When he spoke such words in public, people who owned slaves got angry, and many fights resulted. During one conflict, a man shot Clay, and Clay pulled out a knife and wounded his assailant. Later, Clay discovered that the bullet had harmlessly hit his knife case. Clay said that he spoke out against slavery because it hurt the state's growth. He did not stress how it harmed the people held under slavery.

Another antislavery leader, John G. Fee, truly believed that all men were created equal. Born in Bracken County to slaveholding parents, he went against their beliefs. Fee became a preacher and called for an end to slavery at once. He set up a school in Berea where both races attended classes together. But Fee's actions stirred up anger among those who supported slavery, and they forced Fee and his followers to flee the state. His appeals were among the last in the slave South calling for freedom. Soon the issue would be solved not by words but by war.

Key Political Leaders

Many issues divided the citizens of Kentucky before the Civil War, but slavery brought forth the strongest reactions. Various political leaders tried to keep the sections of the nation together, but they found that increasingly difficult. Across the United States, people saw Kentucky as an important state in the debate over slavery. It had a large population and was a rich farming state during a time when the United States was mostly an agrarian nation. A New York paper said of Kentucky: "The followers of Boone have become breeders of fine stock and cattle that have given them a fame everywhere." The state had more key leaders in national political jobs than at any other time, before or since.

Two of those leaders served as vice president. Richard M. Johnson of Scott County gained acclaim during the War of 1812 because some people said that he had killed the great Indian chief Tecumseh in battle. Later, when he ran for office, voters chanted: "Rumsey Dumpsey, Rumsey Dumpsey, Colonel Johnson killed Tecumseh." The wartime hero was elected vice president of the United States in 1836; he failed in a reelection bid four years later.

The other vice president from Kentucky during this period was John C. Breckinridge of Lexington. His grandfather had been attorney general under President Thomas Jefferson. From his youth, Breckinridge knew that people expected him to do great things, and he did not disappoint them. By the time he was forty years old, the tall and handsome Breckinridge had served in the U.S. House of Representatives and as vice president of the United States, and he had run for president. He is the youngest man ever elected vice president. Breckinridge's only political defeat came in 1860, when he lost the race for president to another man born in Kentucky—Abraham Lincoln.

People wanted a person from Kentucky to run for either president or vice president because of the state's importance and electoral influence.

In fact, in eight of the ten presidential elections immediately preceding the Civil War, someone from Kentucky was a candidate for either president or vice president.

Three times, the Kentuckian running for president was Henry Clay. He lost each time. Still, he is the greatest Kentucky political figure of all time. Clay showed that a person does not have to win to be great; leadership is what matters.

Many other Kentucky leaders won national attention during this period. Linn Boyd lived in the Jackson Purchase area for most of his life and became Speaker of the U.S. House of Representatives just before the Civil War. John J. Crittenden lived in Russellville and Frankfort and had an important and varied career, serving as Kentucky governor, U.S. senator, and attorney general of the United States (twice). Crittenden suggested a compromise to keep the nation together as the Civil War grew near, but his plan failed to win acceptance. As a result, two Kentucky-born men became leaders of the two sides when the war did start.

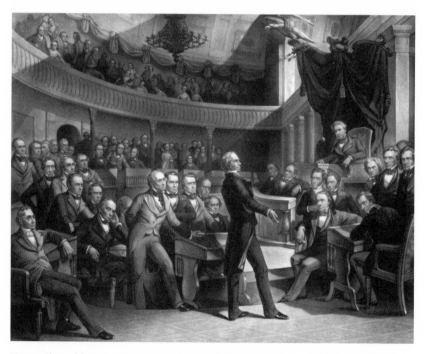

Henry Clay addressing Congress. (Library of Congress Prints and Photographs Division)

Kentucky Lives: Henry Clay

Henry Clay, born in Virginia in 1777, came to Lexington, Kentucky, twenty years later as a lawyer. He married Lucretia Hart, and they had eleven children. However, of their six daughters, all died before their father did. One of their five sons died in the Mexican War, and another spent most of his life in an insane asylum. Clay called his home "Ashland" and enjoyed the time he spent there, despite the sadness associated with the memories of his dead children.

A great orator, Clay became a leader of the nation. On the first day that he stepped onto the floor of the House of Representatives as a member, he was named Speaker of the House. During the War of 1812, he pushed for the war and then helped make the peace that ended it. Later he became a senator.

Clay gained fame for trying to keep North and South from breaking the nation apart. He often suggested compromises to settle disputes between the two groups, earning the title the "Great Compromiser." He spoke for all of America, not just for one section: "I know no South, no North, no East, no West, to which I owe my allegiance. The Union, sir, is my country." During his lifetime, he kept America united.

Three times he ran for president; three times he lost. The last time, only a few more votes would have made him president. Later, when Clay took an unpopular stand, someone observed that it might hurt his chances of winning the presidency if he should run again. Clay replied, "I would rather be right than be president." He knew that compromise was sometimes the best course, but on matters of principle, he must do what he knew was right.

Because of his actions, Clay was more important than many of the presidents of his time. When people were asked to name the five greatest U.S. senators, Henry Clay of Kentucky was chosen as one of them.

Three Kentucky Presidents

No elected president has ever been living in Kentucky at the time of his election. Kentucky can claim close ties to three people who served as president, however. Abraham Lincoln, the sixteenth U.S. president, was born near Hodgenville, Kentucky. Jefferson Davis, who served as president of the Confederacy during the Civil War, was born less than a year earlier than Lincoln and within 100 miles of him. The third person? Zachary Taylor. He is the only one of the three buried in Kentucky, and he lived in the state much longer than either Lincoln or Davis.

Taylor came to Kentucky from Virginia when he was only eight months old. He grew up and married there, and five of his six children were born in the Bluegrass State. His home still stands in Louisville. By the time he was about forty-six years old, he had sold most of his land in Kentucky and moved south. Taylor later became famous as a general in the Mexican War, where his troops called him "Old Rough and Ready." After that conflict ended, people asked him to run for the nation's highest office. Taylor had never even voted before. His first vote was for himself for president in 1848. An open, frank man with common sense, Taylor sometimes stuttered when he spoke, but in those days—before radio or television—few people ever saw a president in person, so few knew. He died while still in office, on July 9, 1850. Taylor is buried in Louisville.

Taylor also played an important role in Jefferson Davis's life, in one of the great romances in Kentucky history. Davis, born in Fairview in Todd County, Kentucky, moved south with his family but came back briefly to attend school in Washington County and then spent part of his college

Kentucky-born Jefferson Davis, president of the Confederacy. (Library of Congress Prints and Photographs Division)

years at Transylvania University in Lexington. Later, he enlisted in the U.S. Army and found himself under the command of Zachary Taylor. Taylor had a pretty young daughter named Sarah Knox Taylor, and she and Davis fell in love. When Davis asked her father for permission to marry her, Taylor refused and had Davis transferred to another army fort, far from Knox (as she was called). But the two sweethearts wrote to each other and agreed to marry when she turned twenty-one. When that time arrived, Davis left the army, and they married at her aunt's house in Louisville.

Seldom were two people so happy. But on their honeymoon in the South, both contracted malaria. At one point, Davis heard his young wife singing and thought that she was better. He got up from his sickbed to be with his bride. She died in his arms. They had been married exactly three months. For eight years, the heartbroken Davis kept to himself, seeing no one other than his family and the slaves on his farm in Mississippi. Finally, he reentered public life and later remarried. During the Mexican War, Davis rejoined the army and fought under his former father-in-law, now a general. After Davis was seriously wounded in a heroic fight, Taylor visited him and said, "My daughter was a better judge of men than I was." They became friends at last, but Taylor died only a few years later. Davis lived on and held several important political jobs. By the time the Civil War loomed, people considered him a good leader for the southern cause. If he took that post, he would have to oppose another Kentucky president—Abraham Lincoln.

Lincoln would lead the Union when the Civil War started; Davis

---

Kentucky Voices

Lincoln's favorite poem was written by William Knox.

'Tis the wink of an eye, 'tis the draught
   of a breath—
From the blossom of health, to the
   paleness of death,
From the gilded saloon to the bier
   and the shroud;
Oh! Why should the spirit of mortal be proud?

would lead the Confederate side. These two men were presidents of opposing sides, but their lives seemed similar in many ways. Both Lincoln and Davis had been born in Kentucky at nearly the same time. Both men married women from Kentucky. Both kept their ties to the state after they left it. Davis did so by attending two Kentucky schools, while Lincoln's three law partners all hailed from Kentucky. His best friend was Joshua Speed, whom he visited at Farmington in Louisville.

Both Davis and Lincoln left the state while still young. One went north and the other south. Both would suffer several political defeats, yet they worked on. Both found out that learning does not end in a classroom. They continued to read and learn after their formal schooling ended. Both men also suffered great family losses. Davis had six children, five of whom died before their mother did. Of Lincoln's four sons, three died before their mother. Both men sought peace: Lincoln wanted peace for a united nation, while Davis sought peace for what he hoped would be a new nation.

Abraham Lincoln, born in 1809, was named for his grandfather, who had been killed by Indians. Lincoln's mother may have been able to read, but she could not write. His father was not poor, as many stories claim, but he did have trouble with the titles to some land he bought in Ken-

Abraham Lincoln with his son Thomas ("Tad"). (Library of Congress Prints and Photographs Division)

tucky, which is probably why he left the state when his son was only seven. Young Abe almost drowned near the family's Knob Creek farm, but a young boy saved him in an almost unnoticed action that would later have a major effect on the nation's history.

The Lincolns moved to Indiana, where Abe's mother died when he was ten. His father remarried another Kentucky woman, and Lincoln loved her deeply. He and his father did not get along, however. Later, Lincoln moved to Illinois and made that state his home. He clerked in a store, ran a grocery, and served as postman. Then he became a lawyer and entered politics. His ideal leader was Henry Clay.

In Illinois, Lincoln met his future wife while she was visiting relatives. Also from Kentucky, Mary Todd was very unlike Lincoln. He was tall—six feet and four inches, a giant for his day; she was short. Lincoln had had only about one year of formal schooling; Mary Todd was one of the best-educated women in America at the time. He was quiet and humble; she had a brash and open manner. Lincoln came from a family

---

Kentucky Lives: Julia Ann H. Tevis

In the nineteenth century, people expected a woman to work mostly as a wife and mother. Only a few other jobs were thought suitable, and one of those jobs was teaching. Julia Tevis taught.

Born in Clark County, Kentucky, she moved with her family to Virginia, then to Washington, D.C. Julia met Methodist preacher John Tevis, and they soon married. The couple returned to Kentucky, and in 1825 Julia set up a school in Shelby County called the Science Hill Female Academy. It soon gained national recognition as a fine school for young women. Unlike most people, Julia Tevis thought that women should be trained to be more than just wives. Her school offered classes in math and science, and she hired teachers who could speak foreign languages and who knew a variety of subjects. Many students came to her school, and just before the Civil War, Science Hill had 230 young women enrolled, most of them from the South. When the Civil War came, however, Tevis supported the North. It was simple, she said: "The Negroes must be freed."

Julia Tevis wrote her story in the book *Sixty Years in a Schoolroom*, published in 1878. Two years later she died. She was a leader in women's education, and her school building still stands in Shelbyville as a reminder of her belief. She said, "Woman's mind is limitless. Help it to grow."

without wealth; Mary Todd came from one with great wealth. He made friends easily; she made enemies easily. They married, and Mary became very important to Lincoln's success. She helped him meet wealthy, important people who could aid Lincoln's political career. Mary Todd Lincoln could also see great things in her husband's future and helped push him to greatness.

Lincoln began to attract attention. This man with black hair and gray eyes was not a great speaker and had little education. However, Lincoln could express himself in writing perhaps better than any other president. He was not rigid in his reactions; Lincoln tried to be flexible and look at each problem separately. When he spoke on the issue of slavery before the Civil War, he saw that it was tearing the nation apart. Lincoln expressed his views clearly: "A house divided against itself cannot stand. I believe this government cannot endure, permanently, half slave and half free. I do not expect the house to fall—but I do expect it will cease to be divided." Years later his leadership kept the house—the nation—together.

All these Kentucky politicians stood large on the national stage—Lincoln, Davis, Taylor, Clay, Breckinridge, and Johnson, among others. They could not prevent the coming of the Civil War, however. Once more Kentucky would become a "dark and bloody ground."

CHAPTER SEVEN

The Civil War and the End
of a Century

Abraham Lincoln took the oath of office as president of the United States in March 1861. By that time, it looked as if there might not be a *united* nation. Many southerners feared the actions President Lincoln might take on several issues, including slavery, and several southern states seceded from the United States and formed the Confederate States of America, or the Confederacy. Efforts at compromise had failed, and war seemed likely.

Which side would Kentucky take? The Washington Monument in the nation's capital bore the inscription, "Kentucky will be the last to give up the union." Would it, though? Conflicting forces tore at the state, as Kentucky had ties to both North and South. A decade before the war, some 160,000 natives of Kentucky were living in the North, and about 108,000 in the South. Although the commonwealth was a slave state, it also had strong business ties to the North. The Ohio River flowed through states free of slavery and into the Mississippi River, which continued south into slave states. Hard choices awaited.

Those choices grew more difficult after the Confederates fired on Fort Sumter in South Carolina, and the war started. Union soldiers at the fort were led by a man from Kentucky, Robert Anderson of Louisville. Although people at the time referred to the war by different names—the War of the Rebellion, the War between the States, and others—most people today call it the Civil War.

Kentucky knew the cost of fighting. It had lost citizens in the frontier period, during the War of 1812, and in the Mexican War. The state of great compromisers such as Henry Clay and John J. Crittenden did not see the need to fight, however, so Kentucky initially took the unusual action of declaring itself neutral. So there existed the United States, the Confederate States, and Kentucky. Lincoln as the U.S. president and Jefferson Davis as the Confederate president knew the potential importance of Kentucky to their respective causes. Each needed his native state to join his side. As Lincoln said, "I think to lose Kentucky is nearly the same as to lose the whole game"—the war.

Part of the reason for Kentucky's importance concerned geography. If Kentucky supported the South, the Ohio River would provide a strong line of defense, since no bridges crossed the river at the time. It would be much harder for Union armies to invade the South if Kentucky became Confederate. The state's sizable population also made it important. As the third largest slave state, if Kentucky supported one side or the other, it could supply many men for that army. Another reason for Kentucky's key role involved its rich agriculture. Its horses could be used by the army, and its crops could feed soldiers. Both sides wanted Kentucky.

For four months, the state stayed neutral. Slowly, it moved closer to the Union cause, and in September 1861, Kentucky made the decision to remain in the Union. Now, individual people in Kentucky had to answer the question, "Who am I, Yankee or Rebel?"

Kentucky Lives: Julia Marcum

In the first year of the Civil War, sixteen-year-old Julia Marcum lived in Tennessee—a Confederate state—but her family supported the Union cause. One day, Confederate soldiers came to her home looking for her Unionist father. When they did not find him, they moved on, but one soldier remained behind. A fight broke out in which he hit Julia in the eye with the bayonet on his rifle. She fought back and struck him with an ax. He then fired his gun and shot off her finger. At that moment, her father rushed in and killed the Confederate. Julia lost the sight in her injured eye. The family fled Tennessee and moved to Casey County and then Pulaski County, Kentucky. Julia's father was later killed in the conflict.

After the Civil War ended, Julia Marcum went back to Tennessee and taught school for a while, but her wounds grew worse. At that time, a soldier injured in the war could apply to the U.S. government for a pension. Julia applied for that support and received it, probably making her the only woman recognized by the U.S. government as having fought in the Civil War—not as a member of an army but as a defender of her home.

Later, Julia Marcum moved to Williamsburg in Whitley County, Kentucky, and died there in 1936, at age ninety-one.

The Brothers' War

Some people who supported the Confederate cause did not agree with Kentucky's decision to remain in the Union. They met at Russellville and set up what they called the Confederate State of Kentucky, with its capital at Bowling Green. That group requested recognition by the Confederacy, and at the end of the year, Kentucky became the thirteenth star in the Confederate flag. However, because Kentucky never officially left the Union, it also had a star in the U.S. flag. Kentucky's representation in both flags illustrated the divisions within the state. People from Kentucky, more than those from any other state, fought each other, and that meant heartbreak.

A woman wrote to a Union leader early in the war, telling him that one of her family members had gone to fight for the South. He would not be the last, she feared, "for there will be many such instances of brothers against each other and father against son." She was correct. It would truly be the Brothers' War for Kentucky.

Kentuckians fought against other Kentuckians at all levels. The state produced sixty-seven Union generals and thirty-eight Confederate ones. Family members chose different sides. Former vice president John C. Breckinridge became a Confederate general. His uncle, a strong supporter of the Union, watched two of his sons ride south and two ride north. One of Senator Crittenden's sons fought as a northern general, and another as a southern one. Even the nation's highest office was not spared these divisions. Mary Todd Lincoln, wife of the Union leader, saw one brother, three half brothers, and three brothers-in-law fight for the South.

Not just the famous families were divided, of course. In an early battle just outside Kentucky, a Confederate soldier brought a wounded Union soldier into camp. Another southern soldier recognized the man—his brother, fighting on the other side. He tried to help him, but the Union brother died that night. The Confederate brother fought on.

Harrison County in central Kentucky exemplified many of the counties in the state. It had about 2,400 men aged twenty-one years and older—of fighting age. Some 1,400 people from that county joined one army or the other—800 fought for the South, and 600 for the North. In one battle in the county, U.S. colonel George W. Berry was wounded, and on the other side of the lines that day stood his son. The son had asked not to fight, knowing that he might be shooting at his father's Union unit. When the son learned of his father's wounds, he went to him, and they reunited amid tears. But the father died six days later. His would be only one of many deaths.

Before the Civil War ended, about 100,000 people from Kentucky fought for the North and about 40,000 for the South. Everyone knew that many of the men would not return, but everyone hoped it would not be their husband, son, or brother who died. A woman wrote that when she watched her brother leave, "I felt as if I would never see him again. I put my face down on the gate and cried with all my heart." Many would shed tears before the war ended.

On the Battlefield

Some 400 battles and small fights took place in Kentucky during the Civil War. Only a few of them could be classified as major battles. After the January 1862 Battle of Mill Springs in south-central Kentucky, Confederates retreated out of the state for a time. They returned that summer in an attempt to capture Kentucky. In August 1862, at the Battle of Richmond, the South won a major victory, and those troops got as far

Drawing of the Battle of Mill Springs in Wayne County. (Courtesy of the Kentucky Historical Society)

as Frankfort, where they placed a Confederate flag over the capitol. That marked the only time in the Civil War that the South seized a Union state capitol. U.S. military forces forced the Confederates to leave only a few hours later, however.

The major battle in the state was also one of the most important in the war. If the Confederates had won, they might have gone on and invaded the North. Geography again played a role. In the hot, dry fall of 1862, the two warring armies needed water to drink and found it near Perryville. Fighting over the water soon expanded into a full-fledged battle. In one day the Union lost about 4,200 men, either dead or wounded. The Confederates lost some 3,400. One person recalled, "The ground was slippery with blood." Neither side had won, but the next day, the Confederates started to retreat from the state. The last major invasion of Kentucky by the South had ended. After that, only smaller raids took place, led by cavalrymen such as General John Hunt Morgan of Lexington.

Whether fighting inside or outside Kentucky, soldiers lived hard lives. First of all, illness and disease struck many. Before the conflict, most of the soldiers had lived on isolated farms and had never been in large groups of people. When they came together in these big armies, they were exposed to many diseases, and significant numbers died. Union

---

Kentucky Voices

One of the important things we can learn from history is perspective. In these two examples, both writers are describing the same soldiers—Confederate John Hunt Morgan's men.

A nineteen-year-old Union girl, Frances Dallam Peters of Lexington, wrote of Morgan's soldiers: "A nasty, dirty looking set they were; wore no uniforms but were dressed in grey. . . . They looked like the tag, rag, & bobtail of the earth and as if they hadn't been near water since Fort Sumter fell."

In contrast, another young girl, Confederate supporter Lizzie Hardin of Harrodsburg, exclaimed: "At last I saw John Morgan! . . . He was exactly my ideal of a dashing cavalryman. Tall and well formed with a very handsome face. . . . His whole dress was scrupulously clean and neat."

Each viewed the soldiers from her own, very different perspective.

Confederate General John Hunt Morgan and his wife Mattie. (Courtesy of the University of Kentucky Special Collections and Archives)

soldier John Tuttle of Wayne County wrote about his feelings: "We buried 11 of our regiment there. It looked a little hard to see the body of a friend of happier times now simply rolled in a blanket, dropped into a shallow hole, and covered with earth." Later, troops marched and slept outside in all kinds of weather, which damaged their health as well. Not much was known about germs, and they often drank impure water that made them sick. In fact, more people died from disease during the Civil War than from bullets.

Being a soldier could be boring. Most of the time, the men marched or stayed in tents in a camp waiting for a battle. They might do military drills, play cards, go to religious services, play baseball, read letters from home, or do other things. Then came the battle.

Many had gone to war filled with excitement. Eager to fight, they wanted to be a part of the conflict. The reality of war soon caused them to change their minds. Union soldier Terah Sampson wrote to his mother in Shelby County to tell her of his brother's death in battle: "I have all ways wanted to see one battlefield and now I have seen it and now I never want to see another one." Later he wrote, "There is no fun in war. . . . It took 4 days to bury the dead." James H. Dorman, a Confederate soldier from Owen County, recalled his days of service: "I was in 42 engagements in all, had comrades killed and wounded from first to last. But I went through them all without a wound. . . . My advice is keep out of war, if you can do so without a sacrifice of principle and honor."

Despite the hardship and death, most soldiers fought on to the end. These men were willing to give their last full measure of devotion to their cause, whether North or South.

One of the most detailed stories was provided by Confederate soldier Edward O. Guerrant of Sharpsburg in Bath County, who kept a daily diary. A teacher before the war, Guerrant joined the army at age twenty-three. He wrote about his feelings during his first battle: "They were men like we that know each other. Never had harmed each other. Personally had nothing against each other. Why [were] *they marching up to kill us?* Strange. No one can fully appreciate this war until he has seen a battle." After less than a year in the army, Guerrant penned, "I want to see no more battle fields. Horses shot dead and the dead and wounded men lying there *alone—alone—alone.*" Later, Guerrant's twenty-four-year-old

---

Kentucky Voices

Twelve-year-old William McChord walked over the Perryville battlefield the day after the fighting ended. He then went to the field hospital. At the time, doctors did not know very much about the causes of disease or infection, so if a soldier suffered a wound in the arm or leg, the doctors would often cut off the extremity. If they did not, the uncontrolled infection from the wound might prove fatal. Young McChord later wrote of the horrors he saw at one of those hospitals:

The house, tents, and yard were full of wounded Federal and Confederate soldiers. I can never forget the groans, wails, and moans of the hundreds of men as they lay side by side, some in the agony of death, some undergoing operations in the corner of the yard. Near the table was a pile of legs and arms, some with shoes on, others with socks, four or five feet high. The dead were in a row 300 feet long, every one with eyes wide open with a vacant stare.

brother was killed. On Christmas Day, Guerrant wrote, "We washed our faces in snow, eat our breakfast off a piece of cold cornbread & beef & waited for the war to close, that's all we have to hope for in this country." Finally, on the last day of April 1865, he and his men marched into Mt. Sterling and surrendered to the Union troops. The Union soldiers had come, wrote Guerrant, "to bury hopes that had been cherished for years, and baptized in the best of blood." Guerrant was one of the lucky ones, for he lived. After the war, he became a doctor, to heal the bodies of the living, and then a preacher, to heal their souls. Guerrant never forgot the war and became a different man because of it.

Guerrillas

On both sides of the conflict, guerrilla groups formed outside of regular army units and would raid and attack the enemy. All too often in Kentucky, however, such groups became lawless bands, taking revenge on their enemies. Others became almost like outlaws, making life a nightmare for Kentucky citizens.

Kentucky had no police force at the time, and many of the men had left their farms and families to fight in the war. As a result, people in small towns and on farms often had little or no protection from the lawless guerrillas, who would help themselves to whatever they wanted. Some robbed banks and stores and killed anyone who tried to stop them. Others burned courthouses—twenty-two were burned during the war. A preacher in Logan County in western Kentucky wrote a year after the war began: "My heart is sad over the evils that threaten us. I fear Ky. will be again the dark & bloody ground. Guerilla bands are hovering over the state."

In Wayne County in south-central Kentucky, lawyer John W. Tuttle recalled how bad things had been: "Lawless bands were continually prowling about through this region of country stealing, robbing, plundering, burning and committing all manner of depredations, cruelties, and atrocities upon helpless and unoffending citizens. . . . The people knew if they shipped one gang out another larger one would come and destroy the town." A captured Union soldier worried about his sister's safety back in Kentucky. "Guerrilla bands are said to be roaming at will through many parts of the state," he wrote.

Some people struck back against the guerrillas with lawless actions of their own. At a time when little official law enforcement existed, personal actions ruled. The lawlessness did not stop when the war ended, either. People had become used to taking personal revenge, and that attitude continued for years.

Results of the War

Many changes resulted from the Civil War. On the positive side, slavery ended. During the war, the Emancipation Proclamation did not affect loyal-state Kentucky. But Lincoln had ordered that African Americans who fought for the North would be free. About half of all the male slaves in Kentucky who could fight did so. Many of them joined the army at Camp Nelson in Jessamine County. In fact, only one other state enrolled more black soldiers than Kentucky did. African Americans fought for their freedom, and they earned it with their blood.

Just before the war ended, the Union also declared that the wives and children of black soldiers would be free. Still, some African Americans remained enslaved at the end of the Civil War. Only with the Thirteenth Amendment to the U.S. Constitution did slavery officially end. Kentucky was one of the last two states where slavery officially existed. But it had ended.

Charles Young, born in Mayslick, was the third African American to graduate from the U.S. Military Academy at West Point. By the time of World War I, he was the highest ranking black officer in the army. (Courtesy of the Kentucky Historical Society)

A second result of the war was that the views of Kentucky and its citizens had changed. Although many people had initially supported the Union, actions by the occupying Union army made some citizens angry. At the same time, as the Union began to free slaves and those in the North began to push for an end to slavery, some Kentuckians objected. Kentucky stood in the unusual position of wanting both a united nation and slavery. By the end of the war, Kentucky had begun to favor the South, and the state became even more southern after the Civil War.

A third result of the war was its effect on the state's economy. A Harrison County man came home from the war and reported, "I found the farm stripped of all livestock. The farm was in very bad condition after four years' neglect." The same thing happened all over Kentucky. The state lost 90,000 horses, 170,000 cattle, and half its mules during the war. It took most people a long time to recover. A few areas escaped such suffering, however. In fact, Louisville, a supply center for the Union army, prospered. After the war, it began to supply the hard-hit South. Businesses in Louisville grew both during and after the war, and the city doubled in size from 1870 to 1900. In most parts of Kentucky, though, the war produced huge problems. Schools, for example, had closed because the teachers had gone to fight. It would take the state a long time to begin to grow again.

A fourth result of the war was that many people died. John Jackman, born in Carroll County, had been a carpenter before the war. He joined a Confederate unit that became known as the Orphan Brigade. During one 120-day period, the group suffered a 97 percent casualty rate; of its 1,512 soldiers, only 50 had not been either wounded or killed over those four months. Jackman told about being hit by a cannon shell: "I thought we were in no great danger from the shells, which were flying over. Suddenly everything got dark, and I became unconscious. When I came to my senses, the first thing that entered my mind was that my head was gone and I put my hand up to [feel] whether it was still on my shoulders." He lived. Later, Jackman wrote about his return home: "Got home about 10 A.M. the 30th of May, having been absent, 3 years, 8 months, and 4 days." At least he made it back. Of the 4,000 men in the Orphan Brigade when the war started, only 600 were alive at the end. The graves of the rest were scattered across the South.

A Union group, the Sixth Kentucky, at one time numbered 937 soldiers. By war's end, half had been killed, wounded, or captured. Almost 20 percent had died of wounds or disease. Even soldiers who survived bore the scars of war, no matter which side they supported. Many returned without an arm or a leg. One man examined thirty-six ex-soldiers in Franklin County and found that they had fifty-two scars from their many wounds.

Overall, perhaps some 30,000 Kentuckians died in the war. To compare that number to a more recent war, about 1,000 people from Kentucky died in the Vietnam War. Civil War deaths touched almost everyone in the state. Few homes did not have—or know—someone who had been killed. Every death was a tragedy.

Martha McDowell Buford had married Willis Field Jones of Woodford County in central Kentucky. When the war started, her husband joined the Confederacy. Her father and three brothers supported the Union. She and her husband exchanged letters during the war, but sometimes five months would pass before a letter was delivered. During that time, Martha did not know whether Willis was dead or alive. About eight months before the war ended, she wrote, "Oh! when will this dreadful strife be ended?" Three weeks later, she told her husband, "The children talk of you so often and are always making preparations for your return." He had written to her, "You know how much or how closely I always remained at home, the dearest place to me on earth, because I had the best wife." Two days after his wife wrote to him, Willis Jones was killed in a battle near Richmond, Virginia. Martha could

Martha McDowell Buford Jones and her husband Willis Field Jones. (Courtesy of the Kentucky Historical Society)

barely live without him. She died a year and a half later at age thirty-seven. Her four children would never forget the effect of the war on their parents.

Another result of the war had to do with those who survived. More than any other state, Kentucky had been divided. Some people forgot the war, made friends with old enemies, and went on with life. But some could never forget, especially when they might walk down the street and see someone who had killed a friend. Those feelings made it hard for Kentucky to follow the first part of its motto: "United we stand; divided we fall." After the war, the state found it hard to be united.

From the End of the Civil War to the Start of a New Century

Many changes took place in Kentucky between the end of the Civil War and the start of the twentieth century. The greatest change concerned those who had been slaves and now were free. The state of Kentucky and many of its citizens did little to help African Americans make that adjustment. Slowly, however, the former slaves began to make new lives. At first, private schools educated the former slaves' children; later, state schools operated for them. In most cases, however, blacks and whites went to different schools, and that would not change for almost a century. African American males got the right to vote soon after the war, and although many southern states kept them from exercising that right, Kentucky did not. That would be important.

Most of all, leaders of the African American community came forth to help blacks move into the twentieth century. Nathaniel Harper of Louisville became the first African American lawyer, and Henry Fitzbutler served as the first black doctor. Dr. Fitzbutler could not use white hospitals and fought such rules all his life. Albert E. Meyzeek of Louisville led several black schools and also showed the unfairness of segregation.

Over time, many African Americans left the state because of the rules that kept the races apart and limited their opportunities. They hoped to find better jobs or more freedom in the North or the West. Some did; some did not. At the same time, the number of immigrants coming to America increased once the Civil War ended. Before the war, many German and Irish immigrants had come to Kentucky, but not many of the new immigrants settled in the state. With few immigrants coming in

Kentucky Lives: Elijah Marrs

Elijah Marrs was born in Shelby County to a free black father and a slave mother, so legally, he was a slave. Still, he learned to read and write at night and in Sunday school. Later, when the Civil War started, he read the newspapers to other slaves so they would know what was going on.

In 1864, at age twenty-four, Elijah led twenty-seven other slaves away from their owners and into the Union army. Marrs "felt freedom" for the first time, and on that first day in the army he wrote, "This is better than slavery." In the army he met the son of his former owner. "We talked freely of old slave times," said Marrs. They parted friends, and the son gave Marrs a box of cigars.

Marrs's army unit moved all around central and south-central Kentucky and even won a few small battles. At one point, the unit was captured by the Confederates, and the men worried that, as former slaves, they might not be treated well, but they were. After their release, Marrs helped lead 750 Bowling Green blacks to the safety and protection of Camp Nelson.

With the war's end, Marrs used the $300 he had saved to start a new life as a free man. Later, Marrs taught school in Simpsonville, New Castle, and LaGrange. Usually, he was the only teacher for 100 to 125 students. He went to college briefly and then decided to start a new college in Kentucky. In 1879 Marrs and his brother began what became known as State University in Louisville. It was the first African American–led college in the state.

Marrs became a Baptist preacher in Louisville and still spoke out for black rights. Freedom had been won, but not equal rights. He died in 1910, still fighting for that goal.

and many blacks leaving, Kentucky's population did not grow as much as other states' did.

The story of what happened in Kentucky during those years has few happy chapters. Farmers faced hard times due to low prices for their crops. Lawlessness led to overcrowded prisons. Railroads crossed the state, bringing both new growth and more control of some areas by the monopolistic railroads. Another conflict—the brief Spanish-American War—took place. A new constitution went into effect. Near the beginning of the twentieth century, some good writers and artists began to achieve some success. But overall, these were not good years for Kentucky, chiefly because of the widespread violence.

Feuds and Murders

Killing went on in Kentucky long after the war ended. At first, the violence seemed aimed mostly at the newly freed slaves as they sought their rights. Soon, however, a different kind of killing emerged. It would gain national attention, and it would hurt the state's image and its growth.

After the Civil War, many feuds took place in eastern Kentucky be-

---

Kentucky Voices

A feud in Rowan County involved the Tollivers on one side and the Martin and Logan families on the other. Several times the governor sent in troops to try to make peace, but nothing worked. In 1887, several more people died in a shoot-out on the streets of Morehead. The General Assembly investigated the matter and reported as follows:

From August, 1884, to June 22d, 1887, there were twenty murders and assassinations in the county and sixteen persons wounded who did not die, and all this in a county whose voting population did not, at any time, exceed eleven hundred; and during this period there was not a single conviction for murder.
. . .
The failure to convict seemed to be that the people were unduly tolerant of crime. . . .

Your committee find that the county officials were not only wholly inefficient, but most of them in the warmest sympathy with crime and criminals. Nor did we find while at Morehead a healthy public sentiment to uphold and sustain the enforcement of the law.

Your committee find—

First. That the county officials are totally corrupt and depraved.

Second. The want of a healthy moral public sentiment.

Third. The portion of the community which seems attached to law and order has been so long domineered over by the criminal element and corrupt officials that they are incapable of rendering any valuable assistance in monitoring the law.

Fourth. The only cure for all the evils that have afflicted Rowan County and disgraced the Commonwealth is the abolition of the county.

By the time the report came out, the feud had pretty much ended, and the General Assembly did not abolish the county. Some years later, the state established Morehead State University in the former feud town.

This photograph of the Hatfield family (of the Hatfield-McCoy feud) was staged by the photographer to play up the violent hillbilly image. (Courtesy of the West Virginia State Archives, Division of Culture and History)

tween various groups or families, particularly in Garrard, Clay, Bell, Perry, Breathitt, Pike, Carter, and Rowan counties. One side generally felt that it could not get justice in the courts because the other side controlled the legal process, so they took revenge outside the law. People killed their enemies, and in some feuds, well over 100 died.

The Hatfield-McCoy feud became better known than the rest. Today, people around the world still refer to it when they talk about one group feuding with another. The McCoys lived in Pike County, Kentucky, and the Hatfields' home lay just across the river in West Virginia. Why the feud started is not clear. Some say it erupted over an argument about a hog, while others point to a failed love affair between a Hatfield and a McCoy. Most agree that it began when some young men from each side got into a fight in which one of the Hatfields died. His family seized three McCoys (the youngest of them a teenager), tied them to bushes, and killed them in revenge. The feud grew from there.

That particular feud did not result in the most deaths, nor did it last

Kentucky Lives: William Goebel

William Goebel's parents were German immigrants, and he spoke only German until he was five years old. The family moved from Pennsylvania to Covington in northern Kentucky. Goebel grew up poor, selling newspapers to help provide food for his family. But he was intelligent and had a strong will to succeed.

Goebel eventually became a lawyer and took many cases in which he helped poor people and opposed big businesses. When he sought political office, he faced some obstacles. Because he was not a particularly good speaker (at the time, a very important attribute for someone running for office), he would do other things to win people's support. For instance, Goebel might promise someone a job in return for that person's vote. Some people did not like his approach. Others liked the fact that Goebel spoke for them. People seemed to either love him or hate him.

In his hometown, Goebel angered one person in particular. He had written some very harsh words about a certain man in a newspaper. One day the two men met and, standing only a few feet apart, they both fired their pistols. No one knows who drew first. Goebel's enemy fell dead with a bullet to the head. An uninjured Goebel had a bullet hole in his coat. The court ruled it self-defense; Goebel's other enemies called it murder.

Four years later, Goebel's party chose him to run for governor. After the election, when the votes were counted, it was too close to call. In fact, initially, his opponent was sworn in as governor, but the General Assembly had the last word on the matter. Most believed that the legislature would rule in favor of Goebel, because his party had a majority of votes there. As the debate over the election was taking place in the Old Capitol in January 1900, Goebel walked toward the building. Shots rang out, and he was hit. Four days later he died, but not before the General Assembly named him the rightful governor. Thus, Goebel became the only governor in U.S. history to die in office as a result of assassination. Several people were arrested for the shooting, but it remains unclear who actually shot him. His death added to Kentucky's bad image.

the longest. But it did get a lot of newspaper coverage, and out of that attention grew the stereotype of the feuding Kentuckian. Such feuds hurt the growth of Kentucky, for people did not want to live or start a busi-

Governor William Goebel.
(Courtesy of the Kentucky
Historical Society)

ness somewhere they did not feel safe. By the twentieth century, most feuds had ended, but the stereotype lives on.

Feuds were not the only kind of violence taking place in Kentucky. In 1900, Kentucky's governor was assassinated, the only time in the nation's history that a governor was killed in office. That event just added to the state's violent image.

As the new century dawned, people hoped that the twentieth century would be better than the last part of the nineteenth.

Thomas Leonidas Crittenden became a Union general in the Civil War, while his brother became a Confederate general; many Kentucky families were divided by the war. (Library of Congress Prints and Photographs Division)

CHAPTER EIGHT

Working in Kentucky

Over the years, Kentucky has been known for producing coal, tobacco, bourbon, horses, and perhaps fried chicken, but is that a true picture of its present-day economy?

Farming

In the early days, most people in Kentucky made their living on farms. On the frontier, almost everyone planted corn, for instance, since it provided food for both people and animals. It also grew tall, which kept the ears of corn beyond the reach of small animals that might try to eat it. Later, farmers began to grow other crops on their farms.

In the years before the Civil War, Kentucky planted many different crops and became one of the richest farming states. In 1840, for example, it ranked first in the United States in the production of wheat and hemp. It ranked second in growing corn and tobacco and fourth in producing rye. Of all the states, only one other had more hogs or mules. Kentucky had a very healthy and varied farming economy.

Hemp served as the main cash crop for Kentucky before the Civil War. At that time, people used the plant to make rough clothing. In addition, they produced hemp bags to ship cotton and hemp rope for use on sailing ships. Kentucky grew more than half the hemp in America. After the Civil War, people began to use metal wire for cotton bales, and steamboats replaced sailing ships. Kentucky continued to grow hemp, however, and by the end of the century, it produced almost all the hemp in the country. But it was a dying crop. In the twentieth century, it disappeared from Kentucky farms, although another variation of it would appear later in the form of marijuana plants.

As the demand for hemp was decreasing, tobacco prices were rising, and Kentucky farmers made the decision to switch crops. Instead of the tall, waving stalks of hemp, tobacco became the main cash crop on Kentucky farms. From 1865 to 1929, Kentucky grew more tobacco

Kentucky Voices

Marmaduke B. Morton, a newspaper reporter, wrote the book *Kentuckians Are Different* in 1938. In it, he described working on a tobacco farm in western Kentucky in the nineteenth century:

None of the modern methods of handling tobacco had been discovered 75 years ago. In the winter the plant beds were burned. The seeds were sown by hand and patted in by dancing over the seed bed so that not one would be left exposed. The plants were generally drawn for [re]planting in June.

We had no planting machines in those days. Plants were drawn from the bed by hand, dropped in the prepared ground by hand, and planted by hand. The planting was a back-breaking job.

The little plants were hoed by hand. When they grew larger they were wormed by hand. When a boy got careless and left a big fat worm, he was sometimes required to bite off the worm's head. Now the use of poison to destroy the worms has lightened his job. Late in the summer or early in the fall, the tobacco was cut and then hung in the barn, where it was either air cured or fired [fire-cured]. When it was dried out, it was stripped [from the stalk]—some mean job.

Then the tobacco was sent to market. By that time, the farmer had to start working on the plant beds for the next crop, for growing tobacco was and is an almost all-year process.

than any other state. It now ranks second to North Carolina in tobacco production.

People used tobacco in the nineteenth century mostly for cigars and chewing tobacco; only in the twentieth century did machine-made cigarettes become more common. On the frontier, people could even use tobacco to pay their taxes. As the demand for tobacco grew, so did the supply. Soon farmers were planting more tobacco than buyers needed. Without any controls or restrictions, prices fell, then rose, then fell again. Earlier, when farmers had grown many different crops, a change in the price of one crop did not matter so much, since the sale of other crops would help even out the difference. Now, with a one-crop economy, farmers had either good years or bad years, depending on the price of tobacco. Finally, the government stepped in and helped bring about steady prices.

In the 1960s, when studies showed that tobacco might be harmful to people's health, the government required that warning labels be placed on cigarettes. States also charged high taxes on tobacco products to discourage people from buying cigarettes. By the early twenty-first century, tobacco's future had become more uncertain, and fewer people were growing it than ever before. It plays a smaller and smaller role in Kentucky's economy.

Another key part of Kentucky agriculture that existed almost from the start of statehood was the horse industry. Kentucky farms had many fine cattle, hogs, and mules, but horses ruled. Before the Civil War, several visitors noted that Kentucky had "the best horses in the United States." Beautiful farms with white fences and horse barns (better built than many houses) soon covered the central Bluegrass area. Great horses, great jockeys, and great races—such as the Kentucky Derby—added to the image. Although other states have tried to take Kentucky's place in the horse world, none has succeeded. Over a ten-year period ending in the 1990s, Kentucky-bred horses won one-third of all major horse races. Kentucky also leads the country in the number of thoroughbred horses (foals) born. Kentucky's reputation as a source of fine horses has long been true, and it remains so today.

What are Kentucky's nonhorse farms like today? As tobacco has declined in importance, the state has begun to grow more varied crops. In 2006, Kentucky crops sold for about $1.82 billion, with tobacco bringing in only one-fifth of that. Producing more income now are hay, corn, and soybeans. Overall, the state ranked twenty-first in terms of the value of its crops. Clearly, farming is not nearly as important in Kentucky as it once was.

Kentucky's leading producer of corn in 2005 was Christian County, followed by Union and Henderson counties, all in western Kentucky. The state's chief tobacco counties were Barren, Mason, and Bourbon. (The state produces about 70 percent of all burley tobacco grown in the United States.) Soybeans are grown chiefly in Henderson, Daviess, and Union counties, all in the western half of the state.

Two important facts should be stressed about Kentucky farms. First of all, the state still has a lot of farms. In 2006, it had more than 84,000 farms—tied for fourth highest in the nation. The average farm size was 163 acres. The second fact is that more and more people who live on those farms make their main living some other way. About half the

---

Kentucky Lives: Caroline Burnam Taylor

In the nineteenth century, some women ran their own small businesses, such as schools, dress stores, or the like. Others might run large farms if their husbands had died.

Caroline "Carrie" Burnam Taylor started a dressmaking business in her home in Bowling Green, and soon she was shipping clothes all over America. Her name came to mean fine clothing. At its peak, her business employed 200 to 300 women to make clothes. More women worked there than at any other place in the state.

Taylor often went overseas to buy material for her dresses and to get ideas for new styles. On one trip, she delayed her return so that she could attend one more fashion show in France. Because of that decision, she missed her ship. It was the *Titanic.*

When Taylor died in 1917, she left an estate worth $250,000 (the equivalent of $4 million or $5 million in today's dollars). The business declined without her, though. Ten years after her death, it closed its doors.

---

farmers work their farms only part-time and have other full-time jobs. Small family farms are becoming fewer and fewer.

Early Business and King Coal

In the nineteenth century, several businesses grew up in Kentucky. Some supplied only a local demand for goods, while others served a much wider market. Ads for Kentucky bourbon appeared as early as 1821, for example, and the state soon became nationally known for that product. Many of the other industries developed along waterways when boats provided the chief means of transporting products to markets.

Clay County in eastern Kentucky, for example, became an early major salt producer, shipping barrels of salt down the Kentucky River for sale in adjacent states. On the Ohio River, other major businesses formed. Owensboro built one of the largest wagon-making areas in the South, and Louisville had the biggest plow factory in the world. The Falls City also had major tobacco and whiskey factories.

Railroads and later interstate highways became important considerations when businesspeople were deciding where to locate. An iron industry developed early, mostly in eastern Kentucky. On the eve of the Civil War, the state was the third leading producer of iron in the nation. That industry did not last long, however. About the time it died out, the timber industry grew up. All over Kentucky, but especially in eastern Kentucky, people cut trees, tied the logs together in huge rafts, and floated them downriver to sawmills. The timber business also declined by the early twentieth century, but it came back by the century's end.

Although eastern Kentucky was often perceived as being rather isolated, through the time of the Civil War, it functioned much like the rest of rural Kentucky. After the war, however, the iron industry died out, then the timber declined, and farming fell from favor. Just then, a new industry grew up that would change the face of the land. "King Coal" began to rule. Coal had been mined as early as the time of statehood, but only for local use or in very small amounts. The first major coalfields in Kentucky arose in the western part of the state, where there were good waterways, better roads, and earlier railroads. More coal came from western Kentucky coalfields than from eastern Kentucky until 1914 and the start of World War I.

Slowly, railroads inched into the eastern mountains, and when they did, a coal boom followed. People came to work the mines, causing

An early coal mine. (Courtesy of the Kentucky Historical Society)

great increases in population. Harlan County tripled in size from 10,000 to 31,000 in only ten years. Those early years were dangerous ones for laborers. During the 1920s, more than 1,614 people died in Kentucky mines from cave-ins or explosions. One blast in a Webster County mine killed 62 people. In 1970, an explosion in a Leslie County mine killed 38 miners, and twenty years later, 10 died in a western Kentucky blast.

Coal has gone through periods of boom and bust. The last boom occurred when overseas oil production halted for a time and the demand for coal increased. As time went on, the coal industry began to use machines to dig the coal, which meant fewer jobs. A lot of the people who had moved into Appalachia to mine coal, or the children of those people, left and went north to find jobs. At one time, more than 60,000 people worked the mines. In 2005, only 17,000 did. Mining remains important, but not nearly as important as before.

Other changes in mining have taken place as well. Early mines were mostly deep shafts dug into the ground. After World War II, people began to mine coal differently. Rather than digging underground, they used large machines to remove a whole hillside—a method called strip mining. Initially, few laws limited strip mining, resulting in large scars on the mountains. In some areas, the practice polluted the water as well. As late as thirty years ago, more than half of eastern Kentucky's coal came from strip mining. More recently, the percentage has been smaller.

Kentucky led the nation in coal production until 1983. Now it ranks third among the states in coal mining. The chief coal counties in 2004 were Pike, Perry, and Knott.

Modern Industries

In the past, people thought of Kentucky as a state whose economy depended on farming and coal mining. Today, Kentucky is more of a manufacturing state that depends on factory products for its wealth. In fact, by the 1990s, manufacturing brought in more than three and a half times as much money to Kentucky as did farming and mining combined.

The change in the economy took place slowly at first. Ashland Oil became a major Kentucky industry by the mid-twentieth century. Steel-rolling mills at Newport and Ashland helped the company grow. Dollar General Stores started in Scottsville and grew from there. The real sym-

Kentucky Lives: Sam Hawkins

Harry Caudill, in the book *The Mountains, the Miner, and the Lord,* tells the story of Sam Hawkins, an African American miner who dug coal out of the hills near Fleming in Letcher County, Kentucky.

The year 1932 was a bad one for Sam Hawkins. The Depression and hard times across the nation meant less work and smaller paychecks. That year, his beloved wife Sadie died. For forty-eight-year-old Sam, the remaining love of his life was his only child, Margaret, who was nineteen. Margaret was attending college at what is now Kentucky State University. Sam could not read, but he had great hope that his daughter's future would be better. Then one day, Margaret wrote to her father (someone else had to read the letter to him) that she was doing well in school, but "it looks like I will have to quit school, though, in a few days. My money is all gone. Unless you can manage to send me ten dollars I will have to come back home."

At that time, $10 seemed like a fortune. Sam could not borrow it, because no one had any money to lend him. He went to his boss, who told him that there was one section of mine that was too dangerous to work, because it might cave in at any time, but if Sam wanted to try it, he could. The pay was 31 cents for every 2,000 pounds of coal he dug. Sam dug tons of coal, alone and under the earth, for almost five hours, then ate a meal. Then he dug more coal for the rest of the night. The walls groaned but held. Twenty hours later, as he came outside to rest for just a moment, the roof of the mine fell with a roar. Sam had mined his coal and survived.

For his work, Sam was paid $11, which he sent to Margaret. She got her college degree, and her proud father saw her come back home to teach. Then tragedy struck again, when Margaret died of disease the next year. Sam never got over his grief.

Harry Caudill wrote at the end of his story: "Sam had put little white markers at the graves of his wife and daughter but no one ever got around to marking his own. Perhaps a coal shovel thrust into the earth like a bayoneted rifle over the bones of a fallen hero would be appropriate for such a man."

Heroes do not have to be famous. They are all around.

bol of change came in the 1950s when General Electric built a factory in Louisville. That factory became the biggest producer of home appliances in the world. Soon after that, IBM built a large factory in Lexington. Manufacturing then began to grow rapidly.

Kentucky now has a varied economy, as shown by a look at the biggest companies in the state. The many large businesses in Louisville include Humana, which is involved in health care; Brown-Forman, which started as a producer of whiskey; Kindred Healthcare; and Yum! Brands, which is in the fast-food business. In Lexington, printers are made by Lexmark; in northern Kentucky, Ashland Oil has its national headquarters, as does Omnicare, a pharmaceutical company.

Yum! Brands in Louisville combines five food chains under it—KFC (Kentucky Fried Chicken), Pizza Hut, Long John Silver's, A&W, and Taco Bell. Papa John's Pizza, Fazoli's, Long John Silver's, and KFC—4 of the top 100 food chains in the United States—started in Kentucky and still have their corporate headquarters in the state. Rally's, Tumbleweed, Rafferty's, Dippin' Dots Ice Cream, and Giovanni's Pizza are all Kentucky-based businesses as well.

Kentucky Lives: Harland Sanders

Colonel Sanders is known all over the world. Wherever people eat Kentucky Fried Chicken, the colonel's white-coated image looks down on them.

The man connected to that successful company was a failure for most of his life. He grew up in Indiana, and his father died when he was six years old. He and his stepfather did not get along, and his stepfather eventually threw him out of the house. Sanders quit school after the sixth grade and worked numerous jobs, without much success. When he was forty years old, he moved to Corbin, Kentucky, where he ran a gas station, but it burned down after a few years. Sanders rebuilt it and added a motel and a place to eat. In that locale, Kentucky Fried Chicken was born, and the good food soon earned Sanders some local fame.

Made a Kentucky colonel by the governor, Colonel Sanders decided to sell his success to others. For a franchising fee, he would let them use his method and his name. Sanders was sixty-six years old when he started what became his great success. Soon he had sold the rights to produce his chicken to 600 establishments across the United States. After eight years, Colonel Sanders sold his business for $2 million plus a sizable annual salary for himself. The business continued to grow, and twenty years later, Kentucky Fried Chicken was sold again, for $840 million. During those years, the colonel gave a lot of money to worthy causes and traveled around the world. He became an image of Kentucky. Sanders died in 1980, at age ninety. His picture and his business live on.

in Europe than any other company. It operates in nearly 200 countries. In the twenty years since UPS first started using Louisville as its hub, the business has grown continually. Louisville now has the tenth busiest air cargo airport in the world. State government employs the most people in Kentucky, but UPS ranks second. It plays a major role in Kentucky life.

A third area where Kentucky has had an impact is in producing energy, especially electricity. In addition to Louisville Gas and Electric, power plants operate near Land between the Lakes; in the Paducah area, an atomic plant produces energy. Because of its production of electricity, Kentucky had the lowest electricity costs in the nation in 2003.

Tourism also gives the Kentucky economy a major boost. Over the past half century, the state has made a strong effort to let people know how beautiful Kentucky is and how much it has to offer to visitors. State parks and comfortable hotels bring many people to Kentucky for vacations. Lakes and rivers provide fishing and boating for both out-of-state visitors and those who live in Kentucky. Many historic buildings and museums draw tourists as well. National forests, a national park at Mammoth Cave, a national historic site at Abraham Lincoln's birth-

Tourists flock to Kentucky parks, like this one on Lake Barkley. (Courtesy of the Kentucky State Parks)

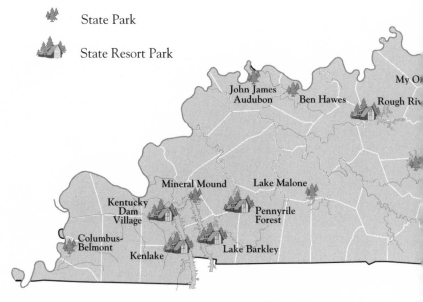

Kentucky state parks and resort areas. (Map by Dick Gilbreath; 2004 data)

Big
Bone
Lick

General Butler

Kincaid
Lake

Greenbo Lake

Blue Licks
Battlefield

Carter Caves

Grayson
Lake

E.P. "Tom" Sawyer

Yatesville
Lake

Taylorsville Lake

Fort Boonesborough

Paintsville
Lake

ucky Home

Old Fort Harrod

Natural
Bridge

Lincoln Homestead

Jenny Wiley

Buckhorn
Lake

Carr
Creek

Lake

Green River Lake

Breaks
Interstate
Park

Levi Jackson
Wilderness Road

General
Burnside

Kingdom Come

Lake Cumberland

Cumberland
Falls

arren River
Lake

Dale Hollow Lake

Pine Mountain

place, the Big South Fork National River and Recreation Area, and a national historical park at Cumberland Gap all bring people to the state. Kentucky is known as a place tourists want to visit.

Global Kentucky

When people grew more crops than their families needed in frontier times, their market was likely limited to other people who lived nearby. Later, they might ship goods across the state or nation to sell. Now, Kentucky's markets exist all over the world. The state is part of a global economy.

More and more, people who work in Kentucky need to know what is happening overseas. In just one example, suppose oil prices in the Middle East go down, causing gasoline prices to fall in the United States. How does that matter to Kentucky's economy? First of all, lower oil prices might mean less demand for coal, which means fewer jobs and less money for Kentucky miners. If oil prices go down, it also means less money for oil-producing countries such as Saudi Arabia. Does that have an effect on Kentucky? Yes. Saudis often buy Kentucky racehorses. In fact, one-fourth of all these horses are sold overseas. If oil producers have less money to spend, they will not bid as high or may not buy at all; lower demand means lower prices to the owners.

However, lower oil prices also mean lower prices at the gas station. This fact could help another group important to Kentucky's economy: tourists. If it costs less to travel, more tourists might come to Kentucky and spend their money there. Also, if gas prices fall, people might buy more vehicles that use more gasoline, and Kentucky makes some of those vehicles. If demand for vehicles goes up as gas prices go down, then more vehicles would be made, and Kentucky workers would earn more money.

Other groups in Kentucky could either gain or lose from a change in Middle East oil prices. Lower prices at the gas station might mean that station owners make smaller profits. Any group that earns less will probably buy fewer items from stores and other businesses across Kentucky, and those businesses, in turn, might earn less. In contrast, lower gasoline prices might mean that it costs less to ship goods from one place to another by truck. This might mean savings for the fast-food businesses in Kentucky, which would earn more and thus have more to spend themselves. Lower gas prices would have an impact on airplanes too. The UPS hub in Louisville could ship things more cheaply, and if other prices stayed the same, UPS would make more money. The examples could go on and on, showing that just one event overseas can have multiple effects on Kentucky's economy. The days when farmers grew their crops, used the products themselves, and cared little about what happened elsewhere in the world are gone.

Kentucky has been exporting more and more products to other countries. Besides horses, the state's main exports include motor vehicles, turbojets, machinery, computers, and chemicals; these products go chiefly to Canada, Mexico, Japan, France, Germany, and the United Kingdom. In 2005, Kentucky sold $14.9 billion worth of goods to other countries, ranking it nineteenth in exports among the states. Most people predict that the figure will grow. The world is now Kentucky's marketplace.

The Louisville UPS hub is a busy stopover for the company's planes. (Courtesy of UPS Creative Media)

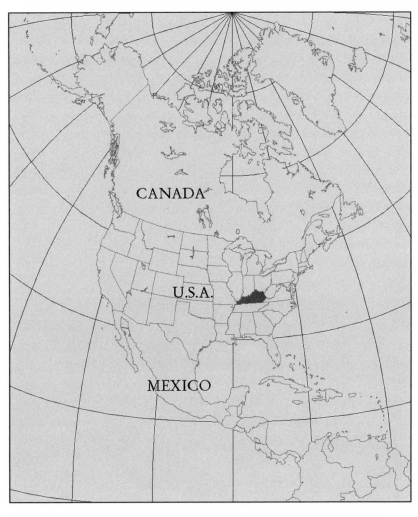

Kentucky's location in the United States and North America. (Map by Dick Gilbreath)

CHAPTER NINE

Words, Music, and More

The value of a state can be judged by many things: its economy, its health care or educational system, its justice administration, or its historical or natural resources. But one of the most important things about a state is its culture. Has a state produced great writers and thinkers? Does it have a strong base in drama, poetry, and newspaper writing? Are there talented performers in the world of music? Is it known for its artists, including folk artists? Has it produced talented actors in the film world?

In fact, Kentucky has done very well in many of these areas. Kentucky's writers, artists, musicians, and actors may not be as well known outside the state as they should be, but in such fields as writing and music, Kentucky has actually outperformed many other states. The commonwealth's culture has been one of its great strengths.

Early Writing

Early Native Americans did not have a written language, so they left little record of their history and hopes. Almost from the time of the first English settlement in Kentucky, however, people such as John Filson began to write books in and about Kentucky. But only after the Civil War did Kentucky's strongest writers emerge.

The first two great Kentucky authors—James Lane Allen of Lexington and John Fox Jr. of Bourbon County—started their writing careers in the late nineteenth and early twentieth centuries. Allen was a teenager when the Civil War raged. After the war, he looked around and saw that the old ways of doing things had ended. But because he liked the ideals of earlier times, he wrote about the frontier or about people in his own era who held on to the virtues of honor and chivalry. Allen was a hard person to like. Strict and formal, he even gave his college graduation speech in Latin instead of English. At age forty-two, he published his first book. His best-selling work, *The Choir Invisible,* came out in 1897. It is the story of a schoolteacher on the frontier and his search for love.

Allen has a female character describe the ideal man: "'I mean,' she said, 'that first of all things in this world, a man must be a man. . . . Then he must be a gentleman—with all the grace, the vigour, the good taste of the mind. And then . . . he must try to live a beautiful life of the spirit.'" Sometimes his books do not end happily, but they present people doing the right thing because of their sense of duty. Allen tried to live up to that ideal.

John Fox Jr. differed greatly from Allen, in that he was friendly and well liked. Fox wrote of the Kentucky mountains, whereas Allen wrote of the central Bluegrass. Fox continued to live in Kentucky, but Allen lived elsewhere after he became a success. Both wrote best-selling books, however. Fox was born in Bourbon County during the Civil War; his father supported the South, and his mother supported the North. Fox graduated from Harvard and turned to writing about the hills, where he had spent so much time. Because Fox could not sleep much at night, he wrote then. During the day, he would eat breakfast at ten o'clock, write letters, have lunch, play golf or cards, visit with girls and dance, and then have a late dinner before going to work.

Fox's two major books became very popular. His first best seller, *The Little Shepherd of Kingdom Come,* appeared in 1903 and would later be made into several different motion pictures. It tells the story of a mountain boy who comes to the Bluegrass, struggles with the love of two girls, and fights in the Civil War. Fox describes the start of the Civil War in divided Kentucky in this fashion: "So, on a gentle April day, when the great news came, it came like a sword that, with one stroke, slashed the State in twain, shearing through the strongest bonds that link one man to another." He writes: "As the nation was rent apart, so was the commonwealth; as the State, so was the county; as the county, the neighborhood; as the neighborhood, the family; and as the family, so brother and brother, father and son." Fox followed his first success with another popular book five years later. *The Trail of the Lonesome Pine* (1908), the story of a mountain girl, a Bluegrass man, their love, feuds, and more, was also depicted on film several times.

At almost the same time, a woman writing in Pewee Valley in Oldham County sold a huge number of books. Annie Fellows Johnston wrote *The Little Colonel* (1905) for younger readers. It too was made into a motion picture. In that book, set after the Civil War, the old colonel's son has been killed fighting for the South, and the colonel's daughter has

Kentucky Lives: Irvin S. Cobb

The stories written by the prolific Irvin S. Cobb have been read by many Americans. He later became an actor for a time. Though neither a great writer nor a great actor, he was very good at both. Cobb was one of the most popular Kentuckians and Americans of his time, and, to many people, Cobb *was* Kentucky.

Cobb was born in 1876 in Paducah in the Jackson Purchase. At age nineteen, he started to work on a newspaper. He wrote in his home city, in Louisville, and in New York City. Cobb's philosophy when it came to writing was unusual. He said: "I have had only three sets of rules: (1) I have never waited for inspiration. (2) I go to my desk at a certain hour. (3) I stay there for a given number of hours."

Whatever he did, it worked. Cobb was a warm, witty man, and people just liked to be around him. He seemed to know all the important people in New York, and they liked his funny stories and sharp comments. His best-selling book, *Speaking of Operations,* told about his stay in a hospital. Cobb wrote that he could not sleep because the nurses and doctors kept waking him up, even though he was sick—"I was not allowed to get lonely." He also noted, "I was not having any more privacy in that hospital than a goldfish." Cobb wrote more than forty other books. His best ones were about a judge he knew back in Paducah, called "Judge Priest" in the novels.

Cobb could not throw off all the harsh views he had grown up with, but he supported more rights for African Americans and for women. He also became very opposed to war after witnessing the horror of World War I. After that war, he went to California and acted in half a dozen motion pictures. Cobb died during another conflict—World War II. At his funeral, a friend noted that Cobb had touched everyone's feelings with his writings and his wit. Cobb's tombstone reads: "Back Home." In what he wrote and who he was, he never left his Kentucky home.

married a Yankee, so he refuses to talk to her. Then he meets his granddaughter, "the Little Colonel," and the youngster helps the family come back together—just as the nation was trying to do at that time.

In 1903, of the ten books on the national best-seller list, five were written by Kentuckians. Later, when a list of the best-selling American books in the first forty years of the twentieth century appeared, Kentucky had the fifth highest number of authors on that list among the fifty states. The next group of Kentucky writers would bring the state even greater national fame.

Twentieth-Century Writers

While most of the early writers had grown up in or near large cities, the next group of great Kentucky writers came from mostly rural or small-town Kentucky. Most were born around the first decade of the twentieth century, and they all helped make Kentucky writing famous around the world.

The first of those writers, Elizabeth Madox Roberts, is now largely forgotten. In her time, however, critics called her one of the greatest American writers. Roberts's first and second books were named the best books published in the United States in the years they appeared. In fact, some call her first novel the greatest work of fiction to come out of Kentucky. Roberts spent her childhood and most of her life in Springfield, Kentucky. Often in ill health, she was confined to a wheelchair for part of the time. She tried to teach, then finally turned to writing. Roberts did not go to college until late in life, but once she did, she gained the courage to write.

Roberts's first book, *The Time of Man* (1926), came out when she was

Author Elizabeth Madox Roberts of Springfield. (Courtesy of the Kentucky Historical Society)

forty-five years old. Most of the earlier Kentucky books featured men as the heroes, but Roberts's book has a heroine—a poor woman. The story of Ellen Chesser in *The Time of Man* shows how strong people can be, even in bad times. Roberts looks at "that proud ghost, the human spirit." Her heroine understands that she has raised a son who wants more than the life she has known. He says: "I want books to know and read over and over. I aim to have some of the wisdom of the world, or as much as ever I can get a hold on. There's a heap of wisdom in books, it's said, . . . and that's what I want to have, or as much as ever I can." The mother is startled by her son's determination, but it makes her happy as well. She knows that he will live a better life. Roberts also wrote one of the best historical novels about the frontier, *The Great Meadow* (1930). However, this woman of quiet courage could not defeat disease, and she wrote for only a dozen years or so. Roberts died at age sixty, just before World War II started.

Many other good Kentucky writers followed her and gained success, starting in the 1930s. Some of them include Cleanth Brooks of Murray, Caroline Gordon of Todd County, Janice Holt Giles of Adair County, Allen Tate of Winchester, A. B. "Bud" Guthrie Jr. and Elizabeth Hardwick of Lexington, and James Still of Knott County. Some of the most powerful writing, however, came from Harriette Simpson Arnow. Born in Wayne County in 1908, she grew up in Burnside. At first, no one supported her desire to write. After her marriage, she began to put pen to paper, but with two small children, Arnow found that the only time she could write was from four o'clock in the morning until seven o'clock, when they got up. In that way, she produced one of the hardest-hitting American novels, *The Dollmaker* (1954). It tells the story of a mountain woman whose family moves to the North to seek work and of the trials and tragedy they face there.

For much of the last half of the twentieth century, the most popular writer among Kentucky readers was probably Jesse Stuart of W-Hollow in Greenup County. The oldest of seven children, Stuart had hoed tobacco by the time he was six and recalled getting only one pair of shoes per year. But he made it to college, then came back to teach for a time. Stuart wrote: "It took life beyond the hills to make one love life among the hills. I had gone beyond the dark hills to taste of life. It was not sweet like life in the hills." He stayed in Kentucky and wrote of his love for his native state:

I take with me Kentucky embedded in my brain and heart
In my flesh and bone and blood,
Since I am of Kentucky
And Kentucky is part of me.

In another poem he wrote:

Kentucky is neither southern, northern, eastern or western,
It is the core of America
If these United States can be called a body,
Kentucky can be called its heart.

Most experts do not consider Stuart's writing as good as that of some of his contemporaries. All of them agree, however, that people like to read Stuart's works.

Most critics would call Robert Penn Warren of Todd County the greatest writer Kentucky has ever produced. In fact, some consider him the greatest *American* writer of the twentieth century. He wrote both fiction and poetry and won major prizes in both. Warren was named the first poet laureate of the United States, a title given to the person considered to be the greatest living American poet. At his death in 1989, most termed him America's greatest writer and poet. Most of "Red" Warren's best books center on Kentucky. These books include *Night Rider* (1939), *World Enough and Time* (1950), *Brother to Dragons* (1953), and *The Cave* (1959). His work usually deals with some human weakness, with the darker side of the human soul. He loved history and saw it as a way for people to plan a better journey to the future. Warren wanted people to understand things past, the places around them, and themselves.

Kentucky Voices

Harlan Hubbard was born in Bellevue in northern Kentucky in 1900. He later lived in New York City and then came back to Fort Thomas. In none of those places did he find happiness, however. After he married at age forty-three, he and his wife, Anna, spent the rest of their lives away from other people—first on a small boat, then in a Payne Hollow house with- ▶

out electricity, phones, or an indoor toilet. They seldom went to a store or left their home. The Hubbards would paint, write, read to each other, and play music together by candlelight each night. Though part of the modern world, they tried to exist as people had lived centuries earlier. Harlan Hubbard kept a daily journal. Here are some excerpts:

July 5, 1932—The most important tie to the world would be art, painting, music, books. Without these my life would be empty and futile.

June 2, 1945—Gardening is a battle. . . . The insects and rabbits feed on our tender plants. A constant struggle is called for to bring in a crop and losses must be counted on, rather than gain.

March 1, 1955—The key to it all is a love of nature, I think . . . I want to feel a touch of the wilderness in the minutest acts. It must be like the air itself.

September 8, 1955—By this time my feet are tough as leather and I can walk anywhere barefoot. Those who are always shod . . . do not know the joy of walking on the earth, feeling the changes in its texture, of wading in the water, of never thinking of what shoes to put on.

August 2, 1956—Caught a young 'possum in the trap last night, had it for dinner. Very good.

July 29, 1961—Sometimes I feel that the whole world is against me, and I have not one friend.

September 7, 1962—Anna's birthday. In honor of the day we had a picnic. . . . We grilled catfish and groundhog. Also had tomatoes and peppers, watermelon and milk.

November 22, 1962—This is Thanksgiving Day. . . . Our dinner was liver, fresh from goat I butchered this morning.

April 21, 1964—Cities are amazing places. Who would choose to live in them, to go to them day after day? They have no beauty; they are without hope.

July 10, 1966—The garden means to us all our vegetables for the whole year. . . . Through the goats, we produce our own milk and meat. Fish from the river and our gleanings from fields and woods make up a good part of our food supply.

Anna Hubbard died in 1986; Harlan died two years later.

Modern Writers

When James Still died in 2001, the last of the noteworthy Kentucky writers of the twentieth century was gone. By then, a whole new group was making a name for Kentucky by their writing. Several of them happened to be in school together in the 1950s at the University of Kentucky—James Baker Hall of Lexington, Gurney Norman of Perry County, Ed McClanahan of Bracken County, Bobbie Ann Mason, and Wendell Berry.

Of that group, Wendell Berry has been called by some the greatest living Kentucky writer. Born in 1934 in Henry County, Berry still lives there and writes his poems and books by hand. He has written novels such as *The Memory of Old Jack* (1974) but is best known for his essays about the world around us. A California newspaper termed his *The Unsettling of America* (1977) "the most important book of the decade."

Berry does not equate all things new with all things good. Nor does he see the past as faultless. But Berry does want people to remember that their place on the earth is but a temporary one, and that they should take care of the world they will leave to others. He emphasizes that each person should be an individual and not "one of the crowd." In his book *A Continuous Harmony* (1972), Berry warns readers to care for the land: "In order to build a road, we destroy several thousand acres of farmland, forever, all in perfect optimism, without regret, believing that we have gained much and lost nothing. In order to build a dam, which like all human things will be temporary, we destroy a virgin stream forever. . . . In order to burn cheap coal, we destroy a mountain forever. Great power has always been blinding to those who wield it." Berry calls for wiser actions and for citizens to remember their place in the world.

There are many other fine Kentucky authors who cover numerous topics and in many different forms. Some, such as George Ella Lyon from Harlan County and Lexington, write excellent children's books. Others, such as Sue Grafton from Louisville, pen best-selling mystery novels. A few, such as Barbara Kingsolver from Nicholas County, write well-received, best-selling books.

Writing History, Poetry, and Drama

Writing can take many forms. While many authors write novels, others write drama, telling their stories in the form of plays to be performed on stage. In the days before television or motion pictures, people saw plays in theaters. In fact, plays were being presented in Kentucky even before statehood. More recently, Actor's Theater in Louisville has become nationally known for offering new stage plays, and Marsha Norman of Louisville has achieved much success in that field.

George C. Wolfe, writer, producer, and director of plays, grew up in Frankfort. (Photography by Julia Maloof; courtesy of George C. Wolfe)

Others direct stage plays rather than write them. George C. Wolfe is probably the best-known living Kentucky stage director. He grew up in Frankfort at a time when African Americans could not go to the same schools or the same movie theaters as whites. On a trip to New York when he was thirteen, he saw some plays, and that inspired him to get into that field. He succeeded and has directed such prize-winning plays as *Jelly's Last Jam* and *Angels in America*. Wolfe recently noted that "the older I get, the more I become Frankfort." As an adult, he found it harder to leave behind the things that had shaped him in his youth.

Another kind of writing is done by historians. Unlike fiction writers, those who write history cannot go beyond the facts. They must find out what happened, understand it, and present it to their readers. There have been many fine writers of history in Kentucky, but the best known was Thomas D. Clark, who died in 2005 at age 101. He grew up poor in Mississippi. As a youth, Clark spoke with ex-slaves and ex–Civil War soldiers. He worked in cotton fields and on Mississippi riverboats. Because he had to help on the farm, Clark did not finish high school until he was twenty-two. Later, he would receive a doctorate in history. When asked about all the history books he wrote, Clark said, "I write because I wanted to write. I did research because I wanted to do it—I found it exciting." Making a new discovery in history could be thrilling, and he tried to give readers that same feeling. "Writing is a lonely business," he

Kentucky Voices

After many Kentuckians died in the Mexican War, Theodore O'Hara wrote a poem to honor them for giving their lives for their country. Even now, people all over the nation still read his poem as they remember the dead from other wars and other conflicts. That poem, "Bivouac of the Dead," includes these words:

> The muffled drum's sad roll has beat
> The soldier's last tattoo:
> No more as life's parade shall meet
> The brave and daring few.
> On Fame's eternal camping-ground
> Their silent tents are spread,
> And glory guards with solemn round
> The bivouac of the dead.

A teacher and a newspaper writer, O'Hara, who fought in both the Mexican War and the Civil War, wrote this poem when he was in his twenties. Some call it the greatest single poem penned by a Kentuckian. O'Hara died at age forty-seven, soon after the Civil War.

wrote, "but I have from the start determined that what I wrote was going to have some style." It did. Clark also helped add to libraries so that others could research and write history. The University of Kentucky, the Kentucky Department for Libraries and Archives, and the Kentucky Historical Society all benefited from Clark's efforts.

A very different way of creating images with words is poetry. Many Kentucky writers of novels also wrote poetry, as did Robert Penn Warren. Others wrote chiefly poems. Joseph S. Cotter of Louisville and Effie Waller Smith of Pike County became the first major black poets in the state, for example. Madison Cawein of Louisville was one of the first state poets to receive national fame for his work. Cawein grew up poor in a German immigrant family. He spent time in the nearby woods, where he learned to love nature. His poems often tell of a fantasy world of elves and mystery, as he tries to forget his own real-world problems. In one he writes of the beauty all around, if people would only listen:

There is no rhyme that is half so sweet
As the song of the wind in the rippling wheat;
There is no metre that's half so fine
As the lilt of the brook under rock and vine;
And the loveliest lyric I ever heard
Was the wildwood strain of a forest bird.

Kentucky Lives: Frank X Walker

Frank X Walker is one of a group of younger poets and artists who try to look at things in new ways. Born in Danville in 1961, he later attended the University of Kentucky, where, inspired by author Gurney Norman, he got his degree in English and art. Walker, the first member of his family to graduate from college, then worked at the Martin Luther King Center at the university and held a similar job at Purdue University. From there, he has done many things. Most of all, however, Walker writes. He stresses that culture can be an important force in overcoming differences. Walker says: "Art is part of the solution. It is the perfect thing to learn to appreciate different cultures, to bring people together. They might all come to the same exhibit, or reading, or pick up the same book. I think that's powerful. I really believe that art has the capacity to induce healing."

Walker's first book of poetry was called *Affrilachia*—combining the words *Africa* and *Appalachia*. In it, he wanted to show what ties the people of the state together. He noted, "My parents were born in Kentucky, both sets of grandparents were born in Kentucky, my great-grandparents were born in Kentucky. Not just me, but there are a lot of people of color who belong to Kentucky, and who Kentucky belongs to." Walker ends his poem "Kentucke" by making that point:

we are the amen
in church hill downs
the mint
in the julep
we put the heat
in the hotbrown
and
gave it color
indeed
some of the bluegrass
is black

Works by Kentucky authors have been printed both inside and outside the state. The University Press of Kentucky is the commonwealth's most famous publisher. In Louisville, the American Printing House for the Blind is the oldest such publisher in the United States and the world's largest printer of books for the blind.

Newspapers

Books, poetry, and drama are not the most commonly read forms of the printed word. That honor falls to newspapers. The first one, the *Kentucke Gazette,* started in 1787—five years before statehood. Since then, many very good newspapers have informed readers what is happening in their hometown, the state, the nation, and the world. The two papers read by more Kentuckians than any others are the *Lexington Herald-Leader* and the *Louisville Courier-Journal.*

The most famous Kentucky editorial writer was Henry Watterson of the *Courier-Journal.* (Watterson Expressway in Louisville is named for him.) He could take a dull fact and write about it in such a way that got people's attention. Watterson could be ahead of his time on some issues and behind the times on other matters. He often made people mad because he openly stated his position. But he made the *Courier-Journal* a very strong paper in the South, and after his death, the Bingham family made the paper even better known across the nation. A 1970 survey ranked the *Courier-Journal* as the third best newspaper in the nation. Four years later, a national magazine placed it in the top ten again. After that, the Binghams sold the newspaper, and its national standing declined.

By contrast, after the *Lexington Herald-Leader* was purchased by an outside group, it became much better. Generally, it boasts the most readers in the central and eastern parts of Kentucky, while people in south-central and western Kentucky read the *Courier-Journal.* In terms of number of readers, the two rank among the top 100 papers in the United States. Newspapers indirectly tied to Cincinnati cover northern Kentucky, while newspapers in Paducah, Owensboro, Frankfort, and other cities focus on their parts of the state.

The highest American prize in the fields of writing, reporting, and related endeavors is the Pulitzer Prize, which many Kentuckians have won. For example, Henry Watterson won the Pulitzer Prize once, and his paper took the award several times later; so too did people connected to the *Herald-Leader*. Reporter Arthur Krock from Glasgow won the Pulitzer Prize four times for his writing outside the state. Moneta Sleet Jr. of Owensboro became the first black American to win the Pulitzer Prize in photography; Marsha Norman won it in drama, as had Kentuckian John Patrick earlier. Robert Penn Warren is the only person in U.S. history who has won the Pulitzer Prize for novels and twice for poetry. A. B. Guthrie Jr. also won it for his writing. In short, Kentucky has produced many prize-winning authors.

Music

Printed books or poems represent the author's words and thoughts. Other people turn their words and thoughts into music. Just as people all over America read the books that people from Kentucky write, so too do many Americans listen to the songs Kentuckians play and sing. The state may not be known for its formal, classical music, but it is famous for its folk, country, and bluegrass music. Its music reaches all the people, not just a few.

When Europeans migrated across the ocean to America, they brought music with them. In frontier areas, settlers passed these songs on to others by singing them from memory, not from books. Over the years, many of these same songs, called folk songs, became a part of the musical traditions of Kentuckians. People such as John Jacob Niles of Louisville and later central Kentucky, Mary Wheeler of Paducah, and Jean Ritchie of Perry County in eastern Kentucky wrote down the words and the music to preserve them for future generations. These songs tell people about families long ago and times long past.

After the frontier period ended, some people began to write new songs and music. In the nineteenth century, the musician most often connected to Kentucky was probably Stephen Collins Foster, who wrote "My Old Kentucky Home." Foster's song "Oh! Susanna" has been called "the birth of pop music," and he produced many other songs that are still sung today. However, Foster actually had very few ties to Kentucky. Later in the same century, sisters Patty and Mildred Hill of Louisville wrote the music for the one song that may be sung more than any other—"Happy Birthday."

In the next century, Kentucky music really began to make its mark on

Kentucky Lives: Loretta Lynn

Loretta Webb Lynn's autobiography, *Coal Miner's Daughter,* tells about her difficult early life. In a song of the same name, she sang:

> I was borned a coal miner's daughter,
> In a cabin on a hill in Butcher Holler
> We were poor, but we had love.

Born in Johnson County in 1935, Loretta was one of eight children and slept on the floor until she was nine years old. "I remember being hungry too much," she writes in her book. She never ate beef until after she married; her family had only pork, opossum, squirrel, and chicken. She first rode in a car when she was twelve, and some of her relatives never traveled more than a dozen miles from home in their lives. In the middle of the twentieth century, she lived first in a log cabin and then in a small frame house with a well out front and an outhouse in the back. From there, she walked two miles to a one-room school, where she got about a fourth-grade education.

Thinking that she could get away from that harsh life, she got married at age fourteen. Four years later—still not much more than a child herself—she had four children. She did not know how to cook, and some of the food she fixed was so bad that her husband threw it outside. Their dog got fat, she notes. Her life remained very hard, and she cried many nights.

One day, her husband bought his now twenty-four-year-old wife a guitar to play, so she could express her feelings through songs. By 1960, when she was twenty-five, she sang at the Grand Ole Opry in Nashville for the first time. Over the next eighteen years, she made forty-six single records, thirty-nine of them hits. She would be the first woman ever named Country Music Entertainer of the Year. Her sister Crystal Gayle also gained fame as a singer.

Although she became a grandmother at the young age of twenty-nine, Loretta Lynn still sang and wrote songs. Often she would start with just a word or a line, and the song would grow from there. Usually she added the music later. However she did it, Loretta Lynn became an important person in the music field. And she certainly made it a long way from Butcher Holler.

the nation. Country music became popular, and Kentuckians stood at the forefront. At least seven people who were born in Kentucky or made their home there have been named to the Country Music Hall of Fame, including "Red" Foley of Madison County; "Pee Wee" King, who lived in Louisville; Merle Travis of Muhlenberg County; "Grandpa" Jones of Henderson County; Loretta Lynn; and the Everly Brothers of Brownie, Kentucky. They came from all parts of the state and won fame in different ways. Red Foley's "Peace in the Valley" became the first gospel song to sell a million records, while Merle Travis won his place in the Hall of Fame as a guitar player. The Everly Brothers mixed country and pop styles.

Kentucky singers continue to be popular in the field of country music. Among those still performing are Wynonna Judd, Billy Ray Cyrus, Ricky Skaggs, the Osborne Brothers, John Michael Montgomery, Dwight Yoakam, and Patty Loveless.

The Country Music Hall of Fame has one other member from Kentucky—a man who created a whole new sound called bluegrass music. Born in Rosine in Ohio County in the western part of the state, Bill Monroe formed his Bluegrass Boys band and made their music popular with songs such as "Blue Moon of Kentucky." Bluegrass music became one of Kentucky's most famous gifts to the national music scene.

Bill Monroe (second from left) of Ohio County made bluegrass music popular. (Courtesy of the Kentucky Historical Society)

At the same time, the state produced some fine musicians in the field of jazz. W. C. Handy, the so-called father of the blues, was not born in Kentucky but said that he learned his music in Henderson. Other jazz musicians include Lionel Hampton, singer Helen Humes, and many others.

In short, music of all kinds has come from Kentucky—folk, gospel, country, bluegrass, and jazz. Music from the South and the North met in the state, and new styles and songs emerged.

Kentucky Voices

The song "Kentucky Rain" became best known when Elvis Presley record-ed it in 1969. The words and music were written by Eddie Rabbit and Dick Heard.

> Seven lonely days
> And a dozen towns ago
> I reached out one night
> And you were gone
> Don't know why you'd run,
> What you're running to or from
> All I know is I want to bring you home
> So I'm walking in the rain,
> Thumbing for a ride
> On this lonely Kentucky backroad
> I've loved you much too long
> And my love's too strong
> To let you go, never knowing
> What went wrong
> Kentucky rain keeps pouring down
> And up ahead's another town
> That I'll go walking thru
> With rain in my shoes,
> Searchin' for you
> In the cold Kentucky rain,
> In the cold Kentucky rain
> Showed your photograph
> To some old gray bearded men
> Sitting on a bench

▶

Outside a gen'ral store
They said "Yes, she's been here"
But their memory wasn't clear
Was it yesterday,
No, wait the day before
So I fin'ly got a ride
With a preacher man who asked
"Where you bound on such a dark afternoon?"
As we drove on thru the rain
As he listened I explained
And he left me with a prayer
That I'd find you

Elvis Presley died on August 16, 1977. At the time, he was scheduled to sing in Rupp Arena in Lexington the next week.

Radio and Television

Part of the reason for people's increased interest in music was the invention of radio and television. One of the pioneers in the field of radio was Nathan Stubblefield of Murray, Kentucky. He did not invent the radio, as some people say. His invention could work only for short distances. Stubblefield was, however, the first person to send human voices through the air rather than over wires, as in the telephone. He set the stage for radio as we know it today.

The first radio station in Kentucky, WHAS, opened in Louisville in 1922 and became the state's major radio station. Soon, others sprang up in Covington, Paducah, Hopkinsville, Lexington, and Ashland. In those early days, before television, family and friends might gather around a radio and listen to programs into the night, such as the "Renfro Valley Barn Dance" from Rockcastle County. For a long time, WHAS played such live music on the air, and its sounds reached many states. But as time went by, live radio performances stopped, and the Louisville station served mainly the city, not the entire state. The change came partly because of television.

The first TV station, WAVE in Louisville, started twenty-six years after the first radio station. For many years, television produced pictures only in black and white, but color images came along in the 1960s.

Visual Arts

People may express their feelings through words on a page or by singing a song, but people can express themselves in other ways as well—by painting, producing films, creating objects for people to look at, or building new buildings. In these areas of the visual arts, fewer Kentuckians have gained fame, but some people have done well.

In the field of art, perhaps the best-known person from Kentucky was Frank Duveneck of Covington. His father died when Frank was only a year old, and when his mother remarried, he took his stepfather's name. Duveneck went to Europe to learn to paint better, and he married an American girl there. She died when she was very young, and the sad Duveneck returned to northern Kentucky to live.

Probably the most popular painter in Kentucky is Paul Sawyier of Frankfort. He studied under Duveneck, but Sawyier never had great success in his lifetime. Part of the time, he lived on a houseboat on the Kentucky River. He would paint a scene and then sell the painting just to get enough money to buy food. Sawyier later moved to New York and died there at the age of fifty-two. In his work, though, he captured the spirit of Kentucky.

Covington's Frank Duveneck painted this young girl in 1891. (Courtesy of the Kentucky Historical Society)

Kentucky has had much more success in the field of folk art. Whereas Sawyier and Duveneck did formal paintings, others learned from family members or local folk artists how to create their art. This kind of folk art may involve carving wood, making pottery, weaving baskets, painting, or quilting. Such art can be passed on from one era to another, just as folk music has been passed down. It may take a lot of skill, even though the result may look rather primitive.

Sculptures have not been one of the state's strong points, but a few sculptors have had success. Perhaps the best of the early sculptors was Enid Yandell of Louisville. An example of her work is the statue of Daniel Boone in Cherokee Park in Louisville. In modern times, Ed Hamilton, also of Louisville, has won national praise for such work as his 1998 "Spirit of Freedom" in Washington, D.C., honoring the black soldiers who fought in the Civil War.

Another form of art is designing and constructing buildings. The state has had some outstanding architects. In earlier times, Gideon Shryock of Lexington designed the beautiful Old Capitol. He was only twenty-five years old when he planned the famous double-curved stairs in that building. The old homes still standing across Kentucky reveal their beauty even yet. From simple log cabins to mansions, each one has a story. But once they are torn down, that story is lost, and their special meaning is gone. In a time of sameness and standardization, Kentucky's challenge in the future is to preserve those older buildings that represent such a special part of the past.

Motion Pictures

By the 1890s, motion pictures had made their way to Kentucky. Those short, silent, black-and-white films provided a new form of entertainment, and people loved them. Almost everyone could afford to go to the movies.

One person from Kentucky had much to do with how moviemaking developed. Some people call D. W. Griffith, who grew up in Oldham County, the greatest motion picture director of all time. He came from a poor family, and to earn money, he acted in plays, worked in a steel factory, sailed on a ship, and performed many other jobs. Once, when he had no money, he got on a freight train and then begged for the funds to get home. Cold and hungry, he returned to Louisville with his feet wrapped in rags for warmth. Griffith overcame his poverty and became the first great movie director. His *Birth of a Nation* is considered the first major film of the modern era, but it included many outdated racial attitudes. However, in other films, he showed a great understanding of people. Griffith himself proved to be a hard person to understand. Although he was a pathbreaking film pioneer, he was virtually forgotten once sound movies came on the scene. He returned to Kentucky and died as he had started life—poor.

Other people from Kentucky went into acting. Some of those with ties to Kentucky include Tom Cruise, George Clooney, Ashley Judd, and many others.

All these people who make up the culture of Kentucky show that the state has many strengths. Yet some people's stereotypes of Kentuckians do not include great writers or even great singers. That aspect of the state deserves more attention and better understanding.

CHAPTER TEN

Kentucky in the Twentieth Century

In addition to the changes in literature, the economy, and education mentioned in other chapters, several other major changes took place in twentieth-century Kentucky.

The Transportation Revolution

In 1900, railroad travel provided the best and fastest way of getting to many places. Kentucky had railroads early. Before the Civil War, railroad tracks connected Louisville to Nashville. Trains could deliver the mail faster, get coal or farm products to market sooner, and take people from place to place three or four times quicker than by horse or stagecoach. As one Lewisburg man recalled, "We had trains, which were the life's blood of all the small towns in Kentucky." The trains were also more comfortable; railroad passengers could eat in fancy dining cars and rest in sleeping cars. Trains gave people more choices. Only one in every six Kentucky counties had railroads, though.

People who lived on large rivers, such as the Ohio, could take advantage of boat travel. The days of the great riverboats had passed, but people could still ship items by water. At a time when few good roads existed, rivers still provided a convenient means of travel.

Thus, those people who lived near a railroad or a river in 1900 had access to good transportation. Those who did not had to travel pretty much as people had done for hundreds of years. They walked, rode horses, or went in wagons. Many people in 1900 Kentucky had only those choices, so it might take them all day to go to the nearest town and back—even in good weather. In the summer, the dirt roads got dusty. In the winter, the roads looked like mud holes.

As the twentieth century wore on, two things changed all that. First, cars began to replace horses. The first automobiles did not go very fast and broke down often on the bad roads, but they still could move faster than horses. Kentucky slowly began to build better roads. In the 1950s,

Old and new forms of transportation meet: a mule pulls a car out of a muddy creek in the 1930s. (Library of Congress Prints and Photographs Division)

the United States started the interstate highway system, allowing people to travel across the country even faster. In Kentucky, major interstates run north and south (I-65, I-71, and I-75) and east and west (I-64 and I-24). Being near an interstate highway was like being near a railroad in earlier days, for people had even faster ways to get from place to place.

Because many towns lay outside the interstate routes, Kentucky built roads resembling the interstates and called them parkways. Initially, people had to pay a fee, or a toll, to travel on these roads, but once the debt incurred to construct them had been paid off, the state eliminated the tolls. Such roads help connect different places in Kentucky and provide the state with a very good transportation system. Some of the major parkways are the Martha Layne Collins (Bluegrass) Parkway, the Hal Rogers (Daniel Boone) Parkway, the Bert T. Combs Mountain Parkway, the Louie Nunn (Cumberland) Parkway, the Wendell Ford Western Kentucky Parkway, the William Natcher (Green River) Parkway, the Audubon Parkway, the Edward T. Breathitt (Pennyrile) Parkway, and the Julian Carroll (Purchase) Parkway. Many other state roads have also been expanded, such as Kentucky 80.

Now a person can drive across the state from east to west (or west to east) in less than a day. In 1900, a trip across the state on horseback or by wagon would take many, many days. Cars gave people the freedom to move, regardless of whether they lived near a railroad or a river. Good roads broke down the regional barriers dividing the state, for people could drive to other parts of the state much more easily. They might shop in a larger city instead of in a country store or go to the city from time to time while still enjoying farm life.

Motor vehicles also changed how people lived their lives. In earlier times, when a young man was interested in a young woman, he would go to her house and they would sit in the living room or on the porch. With cars, young people could leave their homes and go out on dates. For a time, drive-in movies proved popular. Cars made a huge difference in people's lives.

The greatest transportation change, however, came with air travel. After all, people had traveled on the earth for centuries. Horses, railroads, and cars all moved on the ground; they just moved in different ways. When the Wright brothers made their first flight in 1903, something new began. To actually fly filled people with wonder. It freed humans from the ground; they could fly over rivers and mountains—barriers that had always slowed travel. Over time, planes flew faster and became safer.

As cars and planes improved, trains seemed to be forgotten. Now, almost no trains carry people in Kentucky. That age has passed. Today, a person can go around the world in the time it used to take to ride a horse just a few miles. The world now seems much smaller.

Then came space travel in the 1960s. Once more, that represented a great change, since people were no longer limited to the earth. They could leave it and even land on the moon. Most of all, it showed the possibilities for the future. Space travel opened up people's imaginations.

The Communication Revolution

Today, people may hear news on the radio, watch events happen on television, or tune in to a program on the statewide network, Kentucky Educational Television (KET). They might read a newspaper or a magazine or use a computer to get information or even "chat" with other people. The telephone allows people to talk to friends and relatives and

---

Kentucky Voices

The coming of electricity to rural homes changed people's lives. Some women in west Kentucky remembered the change this way:

Mittie Dame of McLean County: "We got electricity and we thought we were living in New York. It was something we never dreamed of."

Irene Taylor of Lewisport: "I remember when we turned those lights on. We just turned them all on and went over the house. You just couldn't believe it was the same place."

Mattie Lou Thrasher of Hancock County: "You put away those kerosene lamps; you put away a lot of labor. You had to fill the lamp at least once a week. And you had to clean the glass chimney. And then we had the light that we could read by, so you could really see something."

Dora Landrum of Ohio County: "One of the great things that hit the farms was the electricity. It just changed everything. . . . The whole countryside was lighted. . . . It was just a big change. Just from coal oil lamps, the old icebox or no ice at all."

Before the New Deal in the 1930s, only 4 percent of farm families had electricity. By the end of the 1940s, some 60 percent did.

---

let them know what is happening where they live. Individuals might send or receive e-mail or pictures over the World Wide Web. Copies of documents can be sent instantly over long distances by fax machines or by computer. Regular mail has become fairly fast as well. But these forms of communication so common today resulted from a revolution in the twentieth century.

In 1900, people on farms were just beginning to get mail delivered to their homes. Before that, to get their letters and packages, they had to go to the nearest post office, which might be many miles away. Newspapers represented the only source of news they had, but because travel took so long, the news might be a day or two old by the time people received the paper. Those near railroads got their news faster. A few of the larger cities had telephones in 1900, but they had no radio, no television, no fax, and no e-mail. Motion pictures had just started, and VCRs and videotapes, CDs, and DVDs did not yet exist. People might play records on a record player, but they had few ways to hear the latest songs or see the newest trends.

People in 1900 often had too little information to help them make choices. Today, society has the opposite problem. Individuals may have too much information, for sources are everywhere. The problem now is how to separate the good information from the worthless and bad. Just because something is written in a book or posted on a computer screen does not mean that the facts or interpretations are correct. The communication revolution has helped people in many ways, but like most change, it has given rise to new issues that must be confronted.

The New Deal

About a third of the way through the twentieth century, the Great Depression struck the United States. As businesses started to lose money, they fired some or all of their workers. Jobless workers bought less, creating problems for other businesses. Without paychecks, some people could not pay off their loans and debts. Some banks had to close their doors, and people's savings, built up over many years, suddenly disappeared. Almost overnight, many people found themselves broke and jobless. It was a hard time.

At the start of the Depression, many people argued that the govern-

Faces of the Great Depression: a Smithland family. (Library of Congress Prints and Photographs Division)

ment should not get involved in economic problems. Soon, however, it became clear that the depths of the Depression demanded a change; otherwise, people might starve or turn to violence. President Franklin D. Roosevelt and Congress started what became known as the New Deal, to help people make it through the Depression. The New Deal also changed the views of many people, who now accepted the view that the government should try to aid people during hard times. For instance, to protect people if a bank closed, the U.S. government guaranteed that their money would be returned—thus the statement that people's deposits are "FDIC insured." The New Deal also set up the Social Security system.

With no work and their money gone, families often had little food. To try to keep people alive until times got better, the government established programs that paid people to do work. Communities around Kentucky still use the structures built by those workers in the 1930s. Many Kentucky courthouses and other public buildings were constructed then, as were schools, bridges, and roads. The gold vault at Fort Knox came about as part of those programs. People who hike or walk in some of the older state parks likely use trails built by New Dealers. In addition, New Deal workers planted many trees across the state. To produce cheap electricity, the government funded the building of the dams that formed Lake Barkley and Kentucky Lake in the western part of the state. As a result, people on farms began to get electric lights and electric appliances for the first time. Those lakes also gave people recreational spots and soon made the area a popular vacation destination.

The New Deal did not solve all the nation's problems, but it helped many people. It did not accept the idea that poor people would always be poor or that hungry children would stay that way. It stressed to Americans that they should try to help one another in times of need. One person wrote that the New Deal "was for a generation of people who had known nothing but poverty an introduction to possibilities." It gave them hope.

Wars

Unfortunately, a series of wars in the twentieth century destroyed not only the hopes of some but also the lives of thousands. In the twentieth century, the United States (and Kentucky) sent soldiers to fight in World

World War I soldier. (Courtesy of the Kentucky Library, Western Kentucky University)

War I, World War II, the Korean War, the Vietnam War, and the Gulf War. Because of those conflicts, the United States was at war for about twenty years of the century.

In the course of these wars, about 12,500 people from Kentucky died, and each family that lost someone suffered deep hurts. Many more suffered wounds, often serious ones. Why did they fight for their country? People went to war to protect American freedom, to aid a friendly country in need, to protect a smaller country from a bigger one that wanted to take it by force, or to fight back when attacked (as at Pearl Harbor). Whatever the reason, America and Kentucky went to war.

In each war, people from Kentucky played an important role. In World War I, for example, the highest-ranking black American soldier was Colonel Charles Young of Mason County. The son of a former slave, he had served in earlier conflicts as well. In that same war, the heroic actions of Willie Sandlin of Buckhorn (and later Leslie County) in eastern Kentucky won him the nation's highest military award, the Medal of Honor.

In World War II, Kentuckians were involved from the beginning to the end. At Pearl Harbor, where the war began for the United States, a navy preacher from Murray, in the Jackson Purchase area, helped out during the surprise attack, and his famous words even became a song: "Praise the Lord and pass the ammunition." Later, when Americans invaded an enemy-held island, nineteen-year-old Franklin R. Sousley of Fleming County was one of the five people who raised the American flag over Iwo Jima in what became a world-famous picture. Sousley just wanted to end the war, marry a girl back home, and start a family, he said. However, he was later killed in the fighting. As one woman wrote of that war: "We know there will be many come back and many that won't."

The same was said of the other wars that followed. During the Vietnam War, for example, the city of Bardstown lost more people, compared to its population, than any other city in America. War took its toll on Kentucky in the twentieth century.

Kentucky Voices

Jim Hamlin was twenty-six years old, and the Great Depression had hit Harlan hard. He could not find work, so he joined the navy. As he noted: "On the application blank, it said, 'Why do you want to join the Navy?' I wrote on there, 'So I can get something to eat.'" On December 7, 1941, he was a sailor on board the battleship *California*, docked at Pearl Harbor in Hawaii.

During the surprise attack that started World War II for the United States, Hamlin's ship was hit by a bomb and sank. In the confusion, the navy lost track of Hamlin and thought that he was dead. A week after the attack, it sent this message to his father:

The Navy Department deeply regrets to inform you that your son James Thomas Hamlin . . . was lost in action in the performance of his duty and in the service of his country. The Department extends to you its sincerest sympathy in your great loss. . . . If remains are recovered they will be interred temporarily in the locality where death occurred.

A service was held for Hamlin in his father's church in Harlan. Hamlin knew nothing about the navy's message or his funeral. Then, on the last day of 1941, his father got another message. It read:

The Navy Department is glad to inform you that your son James Thomas Hamlin, . . . previously reported missing following action, . . . is now reported ▶

to be a survivor. He will doubtless communicate direct with you at an early date informing you as to his welfare and whereabouts. The anxiety caused you [by] *the previous message is deeply regretted.*

Meanwhile, Hamlin fought on. He cried twice during that time: once when he saw the now-rebuilt *California,* and once when he heard a radio playing the state song. As he said later, "When they played 'My Old Kentucky Home,' I bawled like a baby." He came back from the war, alive.

Out-Migration

Another trend for most of the twentieth century was the migration out of the state of many individuals. More people left Kentucky than came to live in the state. As a result, its growth has slowed compared with that of many other states. Men and women left Kentucky for several reasons. African Americans moved north to get away from segregation and to find better jobs. People from Appalachia left after the coal mines

Kentucky Lives: Sarah Gertrude Knott

Many talented people migrated out of Kentucky in the twentieth century. Many others could never really leave the state of their birth.

Sarah Gertrude Knott, born in Ballard County in the Purchase area of Kentucky, went to McCracken County High School and attended Georgetown College, as well as other colleges outside the state. At the start of the Great Depression, she moved to St. Louis, Missouri, where she began a new project. Knott became director of the National Folk Festival at its inception in 1934, and she stayed at her job until 1971. It became her life's work.

The National Folk Festival differed from others in its multicultural aspects. It included both Native Americans and African Americans, for example. Knott began the festival because, she said, "I got sold on the idea of rural drama, of simple natural drama that grew out of the lives of people." Twice the festival met in Kentucky—in Covington and in Florence. By the time Knott reluctantly turned over leadership of the festival to others, folk festivals had moved beyond her vision of them. Like many others, Knott came home again and settled in Princeton, Kentucky. She died in 1984. Her National Folk Festival continues.

stopped hiring. Those who lived in rural areas all over the state simply moved away to seek a better life.

Much of the out-migration took place during World War II and in the twenty-five years after it. In eastern Kentucky, an estimated 750,000 people moved to other states. These numbers are comparable to the great overseas migrations to the New World in an earlier century.

Each migrant meant a great loss for Kentucky. Who knows what strengths these migrants might have brought to Kentucky if they had stayed? More recently, the trend of out-migration has slowed or even reversed at times. The state now offers its citizens fairer treatment and more job choices than before.

Equal Rights

Another trend in the twentieth century and beyond has been to improve the lives of groups of people who did not have equal rights in 1900.

Equal Rights for Women

Women had just started to gain some rights in 1900. As late as 1894, a married woman in Kentucky had almost no rights. She could not keep

Kentucky women called for equal rights early in the twentieth century. Laura Clay is at the center, holding an umbrella. (Courtesy of the University of Kentucky Special Collections and Archives)

any money she earned; it belonged to her husband. Anything she owned at the time of marriage usually became her husband's property. Women in the state could not sit on a jury or vote on most matters. Many people believed that women should stay home and be wives and mothers and do nothing else. Others disagreed. They wanted women to have the same rights under the law as men. They did not say that women should not be wives and mothers; they just wanted women to have a choice.

As early as 1867, a group of women in Glendale in Hardin County became the first to ask for the vote. A few years later, a statewide group formed, the first one in the South. Soon after, Kentucky women asked not just for the vote but for additional rights as well, and they formed the Kentucky Equal Rights Association. Over the years, people such as Josephine Henry of Versailles and Eliza Calvert Obenchain of Bowling Green led the fight for women's rights. Two other Kentucky women became major national as well as state leaders: Laura Clay and Madeline McDowell Breckinridge.

Laura Clay of Lexington was the daughter of antislavery leader Cassius Clay. He divorced Laura's mother and later, at the age of eighty-four, married a fifteen-year-old girl. Clay left Laura's mother little after the divorce, as was standard under Kentucky laws. That caused Laura Clay and her sisters to seek justice for women and try to get the laws changed.

Like Laura Clay, Madeline McDowell Breckinridge of Lexington came from an old Kentucky family. The great-granddaughter of Henry Clay, "Madge" married into the famous Breckinridge family. Her husband's sister was the first female lawyer in the state. So when Madge Breckinridge spoke, people listened. They knew that she was no newcomer; she had the blood of Kentucky in her. Madge had grown up much like other girls of the late nineteenth century. She played tennis, danced, rode horses, and enjoyed life. Then her world changed. She developed a bone disease that caused part of her leg to be amputated. After that, she could have been inactive and lived a quiet life, but she did not. She continued to work hard to get public support for the cause of women's rights and used her family ties to get private support. Breckinridge succeeded in establishing parks and playgrounds for the children of her city. She also pushed the state to pass laws to keep very young children from working. Madge never had any children of her own, but she tried to make a better life for the children of others. In one of her greatest successes, she helped persuade Kentucky to support an amendment to the U.S. Constitution that would give women the right to vote. In 1920, that amendment became the law of the land. At age forty-eight, Madge Breckinridge voted for the first time. It was the only time, however, because she died that same year. But her cause lived on.

In some ways, Kentucky continued to be a leader in women's rights in the South—at least for a time. Mary Elliott Flanery of Catlettsburg became the first woman elected to a state legislature in the South. Katherine Langley of Pike County became one of the first eight women elected to the U.S. Congress. Later, Kentucky would select Martha Layne Collins

---

Kentucky Voices

In 1910, Julia Ewan stood before the other new graduates of Miss Gordon's Training School in Maysville, Kentucky, and asked, "Has Woman Any Longer a Sphere?" She continued:

In the days of our grandmothers, . . . woman certainly had a sphere or orbit, or towpath, or tread way, fixed by imperious custom in which she must walk. . . . She had [few] choices of a career. . . . She could take upon her self the duties of a domestic drudge. . . . She could look pretty. . . .

There were always two possible escapes; the one, an early demise; the other, the finding of a lord and master who, in return for what she was supposed to bring him, was willing to set her over a home of her own, where, second to him, she might rule supreme. . . .

But what a change! What a happy change! . . . Woman is coming to her own. She is crowding into, honoring, filling to the full, and enlarging every calling, from College President to policeman; from land agent to clergy man; from lawyer to laborer; from trained nurse to surgeon. . . . She is bank president, merchant, farmer, editor, sculptor, reporter, lawyer, lobbyist . . . and a thousand other things.

She doesn't loaf; she doesn't swear; she doesn't use tobacco. There is just one thing she doesn't do that she wants to do, and means to do, and probably will do very soon—that is the right to vote, and to have her vote counted. . . . She means to have her rights on this vital point recognized, or know the reason why, and the legal male mind had better sit up and take notice.

Ten years after Ewan gave this talk, women in Kentucky finally got the right to vote.

Governor Martha Layne Collins.
(Courtesy of the Kentucky
Historical Society)

of Shelbyville and Versailles as governor, making her the sixth woman elected to that office in America.

In other areas, however, Kentucky has not been a leader. It has not elected many women to the General Assembly. In 2007 it ranked forty-ninth out of the fifty states in number of female legislators. Comparatively few women own businesses in Kentucky.

Equal Rights for All Races

African Americans sought equal justice under the law as well. In the first half of the twentieth century, Kentucky law and custom kept blacks and whites apart most of the time. Black children and white children might play together when they were young, but by the time they got to high school, their parents would separate them. Black women and men might work in whites' homes and be around whites all day, but such close proximity would not be acceptable outside those homes. Segregation made it a strange time.

African Americans had a second-class status. Though no longer slaves, they still did not have equal rights. By law or local rules, blacks could not eat in the same places as whites; they could not use the same swimming pools or bathrooms; they could not drink out of the same water fountains; they could not sit in the same areas in movie theaters or train stations; they could not use the same parks; they could not go to the same libraries or touch the same books; they could not go to the same schools or churches; they could not play on the same sports teams; they could not use the same hotels; and they could not be buried in the same cemeteries.

One African American man growing up in Louisville during that time recalled, "You couldn't even sit down to eat a White Castle [ham-

---

Kentucky Lives: Blyden Jackson

Blyden Jackson grew up black in the early 1900s in segregated Louisville. In his book *The Waiting Years* (1976), he recalled, "In my Louisville, it was understood that Negroes had a place and should be kept therein." Yet, Jackson said, the ugly, brutal side of segregation was seldom seen in the city.

He was born in Paducah in 1910, where his mother worked in an African American library and his father taught history in the black schools. They moved to Louisville when Blyden was four years old. Jackson's Louisville "was a strong and rich community," despite segregation. People did the best they could with what they had. He remembered good teachers and noble citizens who helped him grow. At the same time, he could never forget that there were two worlds: "Through a veil I could perceive the forbidden city, the Louisville where white folks lived. It was the Louisville of the downtown hotels, the lower floors of the big movie houses, the high schools I read about in the daily newspapers, the restricted haunts I sometimes passed, like white restaurants and country clubs. . . . On my side of the veil everything was black; the homes, the people, the churches, the schools, the Negro park with the Negro park police. . . . I knew there were two Louisvilles and in America, two Americas."

Jackson overcame the handicaps of segregation and in his lifetime saw those barriers slowly break down. He went on to get a doctorate in English and became a college professor, teaching at Fisk University, Southern University, and the University of North Carolina, among other places. He became nationally known and wrote such books as *Black Poetry in America* (1974) and *History of Afro American Literature* (1989). This grandson of slaves became one of the most respected people in his field of study. Blyden Jackson died in 2000 at age eighty-nine.

burger]. You had to buy the White Castle from the take-out window." Another man from Paducah told how white boys and black boys "shot at birds together. We played marbles together, and ball. Why did we have to go to different schools? I couldn't quite understand it." He could not understand it because he believed that American democracy meant that all are created equal.

Eventually, more and more black and white people began to question the rules of segregation. In the 1930s, voters elected Charles W. Anderson Jr. of Louisville to the General Assembly; he was the first African American to hold that office in Kentucky and the first black man to serve as a legislator in the South in the twentieth century. It came about because African Americans in the state continued to vote, unlike their situation in the Deep South.

Finally, in 1954, the U.S. Supreme Court ruled that segregation must end. Although many people in the southern states resisted and tried to fight the ruling, Kentucky was seen as a model for the South. In the next

Martin Luther King Jr. leads a civil rights march in Frankfort in 1964. (Copyright by the *Louisville Courier-Journal*)

year, black students entered previously all-white schools in Lexington and Wayne County, and the integration process had started. People at Clay in Webster County and Sturgis in Union County protested, trying to keep segregation. The governor sent in troops and stopped their actions. After that, across Kentucky, change took place quietly in the schools.

It took longer for segregation to end in other areas. Black students would "sit in" at lunch counters to protest not being able to eat there, and although the owners usually gave in and served them, stronger laws were needed. In 1964, Martin Luther King Jr. came to Kentucky to lead a march of more than 10,000 people to the state capitol to plead for such a law. The General Assembly failed to pass the law then, but two years later it enacted the Civil Rights Act, the first such state law in the South.

Several black leaders spoke out for the cause in the state. Frank Stanley Jr. of the black newspaper the *Louisville Defender* told of the need for change, and Luska J. Twyman of Glasgow became the first African American mayor elected to a full term in a Kentucky city. At the national level, Whitney Young Jr. of Shelby County served as head of the Urban League, a group that pushed for black rights and called for understanding between the races. Because of Young's work, the president of the United States awarded him the nation's highest nonmilitary honor.

Probably the best-known Kentuckian of the 1960s and 1970s was not Young or even some white person. It was an African American man who bore the same name as the early antislavery leader Cassius Clay. He later joined another religion and changed his name: Cassius Clay became Muhammad Ali. Ali grew up in Louisville and in 1960 won an Olympic gold medal in boxing. He got so upset about segregation, though, that he later threw his medal in the Ohio River. Ali became heavyweight champion of the world in 1964 but had to give up the title three years later when he refused induction into the army, based on his religious beliefs. The U.S. Supreme Court later supported his stand. After that, he won the title two more times, in 1974 and in 1978, and became world famous. More recently, he has made peace with the city where he threw away his medal, and Louisville has honored him in several ways, including a museum named for him.

Those changes in the city's treatment of Ali—from segregating him to honoring him—show how the state has changed over the past fifty years. Things that could not have happened half a century ago now hap-

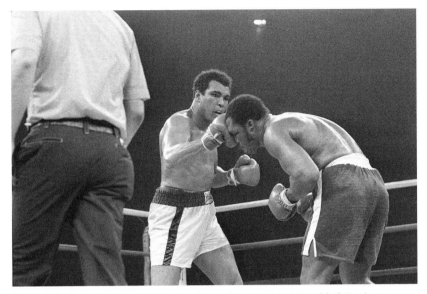

Boxer Muhammad Ali in a 1975 fight. (Courtesy of AP/Wide World Photos)

pen every day in Kentucky, and hardly anyone thinks anything about it. It now seems natural for blacks and whites to eat together, swim together, and go to the same movies, libraries, parks, and hotels. Some people still judge others by their skin color, however, and new groups, such as Hispanics, face some of those same old problems. Kentucky has come a long way, but it still has a long way to go before it achieves the American ideal.

Politics

The last major change in twentieth-century Kentucky involves politics. A chart of which political party won Kentucky elections in the twentieth century would look like a roller coaster. Some counties tend to vote consistently for one party, and some for another. Only a few divide fairly evenly. However, looking at elections to the General Assembly over the entire twentieth century, Democrats generally won those races, as well as many local ones. For much of the twentieth century, Kentucky was solidly a Democratic state, but that changed near the century's end.

In the governor's races, in the first third of the century, the two parties almost evenly divided that office. The Great Depression and its effects, however, caused some—particularly blacks and laborers—to move from the Republican to the Democratic Party. That changed the balance. In fact, before 2003, Democrats had been elected governor fifty-two of the last fifty-six years. In 2003, Republicans won the governorship for the first time in thirty-six years, but lost the office four years later.

In federal elections for president, U.S. senators, and U.S. representatives, a very different trend can be seen. Over the last fifty years, the two parties have divided Senate seats and votes for president. Democrats tended to win most House elections for the first part of that period; more recently, Republicans have won most of them. In short, Kentucky has been divided. It has favored one party, then the other party, and has gone back and forth in how it votes.

One thing that has remained the same across the years has been the presence of strong leaders in both parties. In the last half century, for example, Republicans elected Senator John Sherman Cooper of Somerset to numerous terms. In 1960, national newspaper reporters named him the best Republican senator in Washington, D.C. Besides Governor Louie Nunn, another recent Republican leader has been Senator Mitch McConnell of Louisville.

The best-known Democratic leaders have included A. B. "Happy" Chandler, who was born in Corydon in western Kentucky and lived in Versailles in the central Bluegrass. In addition to serving as governor and U.S. senator, he was the commissioner of major league baseball for a time. Twenty years after he first won the governor's race, he won again, using the slogan "Be like your pappy, and vote for Happy." Other Democratic leaders include Alben W. Barkley; Governor and Senator Earle

Kentucky Lives: Alben W. Barkley

Named Willie Alben Barkley by his parents, the young Barkley decided that Alben W. Barkley was a better name for a budding politician. Born in a log house in Graves County in the Purchase area of Kentucky, Barkley later made his home in Paducah and rose to political greatness from there. During his entire career, he lost only one race—for governor in 1923. After that, he became the most important Kentucky political figure of the twentieth century.

Barkley served fourteen years in the U.S. House of Representatives and ▶

then twenty-four years in the U.S. Senate. During part of that time, he held the key job of majority leader of the Senate. In that post, he helped get important New Deal and wartime acts passed. Later, when he became vice president under President Harry Truman, people called him the "Veep."

Barkley might have been president if he had not held so fast to his beliefs. In 1944, President Franklin D. Roosevelt sent a tax bill to the Senate. Barkley finally got the bill passed after having to accept many amendments to it. Roosevelt then vetoed the bill, and Barkley felt betrayed; he had done the best he could, and the president had not supported him. In protest, he resigned as majority leader, but the senators reelected him the next day and passed the bill over the president's veto. Barkley had done "what he thought . . . honor required." However, that action angered Roosevelt. Barkley had been a leading choice to be vice president, but Roosevelt picked Harry S. Truman instead. Only months after the election, Roosevelt died, and Truman became president. But it could have been Barkley.

Barkley continued to serve the nation well. Witty and warm, he was an excellent speaker. One man who heard him recalled, "He was nearly irresistible. When he got going [as a speaker] he carried everything with him like a windstorm." Senator Barkley was giving a speech at a college in 1956, and he ended with these words: "I would rather be a servant in the house of the Lord, than sit in the seats of the mighty." He then fell over dead from a heart attack. But those last words would become some of the most famous in Kentucky history. Barkley had died as a servant of the people of the state.

Vice President Alben Barkley (right) of Paducah, with President Harry Truman. (Courtesy of the Kentucky Library, Western Kentucky University)

Clements of Union County, the first modern governor of the state; Bert Combs; and Wendell Ford of Owensboro. After being governor, Ford entered the U.S. Senate and held several key posts there. When Ford left the Senate, he had served there longer than any other Kentuckian.

Kentucky's Best Year

For Kentucky, perhaps the best year of the twentieth century was 1949. In terms of politics, that was when President Harry Truman was inaugurated for a second term. His grandparents came from Kentucky. Swearing him in was Chief Justice Fred Vinson—from Kentucky. The vice president taking the oath of office was Alben Barkley—of Kentucky. He was sworn in by another Supreme Court justice, Stanley Reed—of Kentucky. Yet another Kentucky-born justice watched.

In sports that same year, Adolph Rupp of the University of Kentucky won another basketball championship, and a horse from Calumet Farm of Lexington won the Kentucky Derby. In professional basketball, Joe Fulks from Marshall County set a new record by scoring sixty-three points in one game. Baseball's "Pee Wee" Reese of Kentucky led his team into the World Series.

In the arts, Kentuckian Robert Penn Warren saw a movie based on one of his books win the Academy Award for best movie of the year. Covington-born Robert Surtees won an Oscar as well for his filming of another movie. In Lexington, A. B. Guthrie's second book came out that year and won the Pulitzer Prize a year later. Another movie of 1949 starred actor John Wayne as "The Fighting Kentuckian." Kentucky seemed to be everywhere a person looked.

When the twentieth century ended, people could look back and see that much had changed. Some have said that more changes took place in the twentieth century than in all the centuries before. Whether that is true or not, a person born in the first decade of the twentieth century who was still alive in the last year of that century had witnessed vast changes. And the lifetimes of their grandchildren seemed likely to hold even more.

CHAPTER ELEVEN

Going to School

Early Kentucky Schools

One historian wrote that frontier Kentucky "was a battlefield not a schoolground." Frontier people had to fight for their lives, so setting up schools did not seem so important. Yet, almost from the first year of the settlements, teachers taught students in forts and then in rough schools. People valued education, even with danger all around them.

At that time, most people believed that education should be a private matter. Even after Kentucky became a state, legislators did not think the state should pay for schools, except in a very indirect way—a view that held Kentucky education back. Instead, they set up private schools called academies. Students who attended these academies had to pay tuition. The state encouraged these schools by giving them land that they could sell, using the funds to support the school. Probably about 250 such schools were begun in a 100-year period. The plan did not work very well, however. Many of the academies went broke and closed, while others provided only a weak education. In addition, most people could not afford to pay to send their children to school. In fact, nearly forty years after Kentucky became a state, fewer than one in five children went to any school at all. If the state wanted its future citizens to be educated, something different had to be done.

While Kentuckians sought an answer to the problem, private groups opened their own schools. Soon after statehood, a Lexington paper noted in 1798 that a Sunday school would be opened "for the use of the People of Color. Those who wish their servants taught, will please send a line." Unlike most other slave states, Kentucky did not keep slaves from learning to read and write. This was one of the few schools for African Americans.

At the same time, schools for girls opened up as well, such as Julia Tevis's. Catholic groups also started female academies in Nelson and Marion counties, the first such schools west of the mountains. Other

Kentucky Voices

The Reverend J. J. Bullock guided the new public school system at its beginning in 1838. The twenty-six-year-old Bullock left after a year due to poor health, but when he recovered, he went back to preaching and later became the chief minister to the U.S. Senate. His first report to the General Assembly explained why public schools should be well funded:

The great object of the Common School law is to give every child in the Commonwealth a good common school education; to develop the whole intellect of the State. The great principle of the System is that of equality; the rich and the poor are placed on the same footing. . . .

That the education of all the children of the State will cost much, I do not wish to conceal; but it should be obtained at any cost. . . . Nothing is so wasteful as ignorance. . . . The elevation of an entire people is beyond all price. . . .

To provide for the education of all the children in the State is the most economical expenditure of money that can possibly be made. Ignorance keeps inactive the mind . . . and leads inevitably to poverty.

schools for young women were established over time, such as Potter College in Bowling Green.

Still, these schools served only a small portion of the school-aged children in the state. Finally, in 1838, Kentucky set up a system of public schools. The U.S. government had surplus funds that it sent back to the states. Kentucky pledged to "forever" use that money to fund and sustain a general system of public instruction.

About ten years later, the Reverend Robert J. Breckinridge of Danville and Lexington served as superintendent of public instruction, in charge of Kentucky schools. He discovered that few schools had been set up and few children went to school. A typical school was open for only three months of the year, and with fifty students and one teacher, it could expect a total of only $15 in annual state aid. That was not enough. Breckinridge successfully pushed for a tax to provide the necessary money. He then started more schools. When he left office, nine of every ten children went to school, at least part-time. Most of all, he made people believe "that the work can be done and shall be done." Breckinridge came to be known as the "father of Kentucky public schools."

Life in School

Most children in Kentucky went to one-room schools. As late as 1920, about 7,000 of the 8,000 elementary schools in the state still had only one room. That meant they also had only one teacher. The children would take turns working with the teacher. If lessons were done out loud, everyone could hear what was said.

Daniel Drake of Mason County went to an early frontier school. It was sixteen feet wide and twenty feet long and was made of logs. The spaces between the logs were poorly filled and failed to keep out the wind and cold. One boy recalled that "the ink cannot be kept from freezing." The only light in Drake's one-room school came through holes covered with oiled paper, since there was no window glass. Water had to be brought from a stream 300 yards away. Drake remembered that his poorly trained teacher could instruct in spelling, reading, and a bit of writing, but little else.

School buildings changed very little over the decades. A few years after the Civil War, a Kentucky governor described the average schoolhouse: "A little, square, squatty, unhewed log building, blazing in the

Interior of a rural school in Leslie County in the 1930s. (Courtesy of the University of Kentucky Special Collections and Archives)

sun, standing upon the dusty highway or some bleak and barren spot that has been robbed of every tree and blossoming shrub, without yard, fence, or other surroundings suggestive of comfort . . . is the fit representative of the district schoolhouses of the Commonwealth." He continued: "The benches [were] slabs with legs in them so long as to lift the little fellows' feet from the floor, and without support for the back." The governor called them places "full of foul air." The lack of funding, he noted, "condemns childhood to pass its bright young days." The governor went on to say that such a school "seems to have been built simply for a pen for prisoners, at the smallest outlay of money, labor, or skill. . . . It stands an offense to justice, kindness, taste, . . . [a] blot upon the site."

The lack of proper funding continued for nearly a century after that governor's observations. In fact, about twenty years later, a man wrote of the problems he faced: "The difficulty I meet in the work of improving our [school] house is to get the people to understand that a Wood-

---

Kentucky Voices

In 1921, the Kentucky Education Commission gave its report on the state's schools. It had this to say about the buildings:

The great majority of rural schoolhouses—approximately 9 out of 10—are one-room, box-like structures . . . [and] have in the main, a single classroom. . . .

Approximately 50 percent of these schoolhouses are painted and in good repair. . . . The other half in most instances never had even an initial coat of paint, and are in ill repair. The roofs leak, the weather boarding is off here and there; doors are broken, knobs gone, window panes out, walls stained, floors uneven and cracked, seats broken and out of place, and a pall of dust over all.

A stove furnishes heat, the fire being started by the first person who reaches school. . . . A galvanized bucket with the common drinking cup almost invariably takes the place of a sanitary drinking fountain; lavatory facilities are nonexistent. The blackboard usually consists of a front wall and a few side walls painted black. . . .

About half of the rural schools have wells or cisterns; at the other half, water is carried from a nearby spring or well. . . .

Of the city school buildings, 40 percent are old structures. . . . They are, as a rule, inadequately lighted and ventilated.

ford County child is worth as much as a race horse and is entitled to as good a home." About forty years after that, another man wrote that the problem still existed: "Apparently Kentuckians are building $500 school houses along million dollar highways." He noted that every other state in the Union had spent more on school buildings from 1920 to 1930 than Kentucky had.

So, throughout much of the state's history, children went to schools that were not supported at the level they should have been. But what was a typical day like in those schools of about a century ago? One man in the Purchase area recalled that his school day lasted from eight in the morning to four in the afternoon. Students had morning and afternoon recess and an hour for lunch and more play. In his school, everyone read out loud, and each student learned some things well but other subjects not at all. He noted that in geography he learned the names of the states and countries "but knew nothing about people and their ways of living" in those places.

A few years later, a Lyon County man described his school experiences. His father bought him clothes for the year—two pairs of overalls and two blue shirts. The student did not need shoes yet, for everyone went barefoot until the first frost came. His school year ran for seven months, from July through January. The school day started at eight, with a twenty-minute morning recess and then an hour for lunch. The

Early-twentieth-century students walking to school. (Courtesy of the Kentucky Historical Society)

children brought their own lunch, usually carried in a lard bucket, shoe box, paper sack, or, later, lunch pail or bucket. After lunch, they went back to classes until school let out at three.

In the 1920s, Lyde Simpson went to a small school in Jessamine County in central Kentucky. She remembered, "We had 18 to 23 students in all eight grades, only about two or three per class. School lasted from 8:30 in the morning until 3:00 in the afternoon. Most students walked to school; some rode horses. The building was heated by an old coal and wood stove. There was a well. We would draw water from it and use tin cups or a dipper to drink from. For lunch we brought sack lunches."

A teacher in that same school recalled that before she came, "Several teachers had been driven off from there. The students had the reputation of being a wild bunch, and the teachers couldn't manage them." Other teachers in other schools across the state told similar stories of violence and of students bringing guns and knives to school— unfortunately, a problem that is still with us.

Teachers more than earned their meager pay. The average teacher received $215 a year in 1900, $340 in 1910, and $410 in 1920. The Jessamine County schoolteacher mentioned earlier earned $72 a month for a seven-month school term, or a little over $500 a year in 1925. At that time, a cheap new car cost $800. Now, most teachers' annual salaries are more than the cost of a new car. The first person to head the Kentucky school system wrote that for the teaching profession to attract and retain good people, it would have to offer more than a person could earn working on a farm. For a long time, that was not the case. Their salaries have gone up, but for many years, Kentucky teachers were not well paid.

In those early days, teachers also "boarded around." Local families would take turns providing teachers with room and board. The teacher would live with one family for a month, and then move in with another family. That helped teachers save money and encouraged them to stay in the profession.

Still, teaching meant hard work and low pay. One person said that teachers needed only a few things to run a school—a bell, a water bucket, a blackboard, and a stove. He forgot to mention a love for children, knowledge of the subjects, and a lot more. Teachers had to start the fire in the morning and clean the building after the children left. Most of them taught by themselves in a one-room school with students of various ages. Despite all the problems, many teachers taught well, and learning did take place. A good teacher and willing students can overcome many problems.

Special Schools

Certain groups supported schools with different purposes. For instance, at Great Crossing in Scott County, Choctaw Academy, a school for Indians, opened in 1825 and had students for twenty-three years. The Choctaw tribal nations provided funds to support the school, but Native Americans from many other tribal groups attended too. One odd thing about the school is that it was operated under the auspices of future vice president Richard M. Johnson, who had gained fame for his killing of the Native American chief Tecumseh.

Some years before Kentucky supported free public schools for all children, it began to support a school to help educate hearing-impaired

Kentucky Lives: Cora Wilson Stewart

In 1900, one out of every six people in Kentucky could not read or write. In the prisons, six out of ten were illiterate. Cora Wilson Stewart saw this as a real problem, and she tried to do something about it.

Stewart grew up in Rowan County and began teaching school at age twenty. Six years later, she was in charge of the whole county school system. She also became the first female president of the state teachers' organization. Stewart decided to start night schools to teach adults how to read and write. She called them Moonlight Schools because, after a day's work, people walked or rode to school by the light of the moon. Stewart also wrote a series of textbooks for these schools, and she became a world-famous speaker on the subject of education for adults.

Stewart's success won her much praise. For six years, the state gave her group money to expand the popular Moonlight Schools all over the state. But then the funds stopped, and it became more difficult to continue. Because of her efforts, Kentucky was, for a time, a leader in helping adults learn to read and write. By 1940, however, only one state had a higher percentage of citizens who were illiterate. When Stewart died in 1958, she knew that the fight for education would have to go on.

children. In 1823, the Kentucky School for the Deaf in Danville became the first state-supported school of its kind in the United States. Less than twenty years later, Kentucky also set up a school for the visually impaired. The Kentucky School for the Blind in Louisville was the third state-supported school for the blind in the nation and the sixth such school overall. Kentucky led in those areas.

Church-supported or independently supported settlement schools started near the end of the nineteenth century. In many parts of Kentucky, especially the eastern region, these were the first schools people had. The settlement school workers not only taught school subjects but also helped people learn other useful things. Some of the best-known settlement schools were Hindman in Knott County, Pine Mountain in Harlan County, and what became Alice Lloyd College in Knott County. At a time when few public schools existed in some parts of the state, these schools met a need. Later, most settlement schools became part of the public school system, closed, or changed in other ways, but for a time, they played an important role in Kentucky education.

Schools in the Twentieth Century and Beyond

For students in elementary, middle, and high schools, the twentieth century offered a mixed record. In the first half of the century, schools fared poorly. Toward the end of the century, things got better. By then, however, the state had fallen far behind, and catching up with other states would take time.

In 1900, Kentucky seemed to be well situated educationally. The state ranked high among southern states in the number of people who could read and write, the length of the school year, and the amount of money it spent per schoolchild. As the century went on, however, the state dropped further behind. That trend continued for a long time, and the hopes of 1900 faded.

Three major events took place in Kentucky education in the twentieth century, and the effects from all three remain. Although they all helped the state's schools move forward, there was more to be done. The first main change in Kentucky schools came in 1908, when the General Assembly passed a law that improved the whole educational system. It declared that every county in the state must set up a public high school within its borders. In addition, tax money would be provided to the schools, giving them five times the funding they had received before. The act also strengthened the compulsory education law.

Education professionals knew that the people of Kentucky needed to support the law year after year, so they carried out what they called the Whirlwind Campaign. Like a whirlwind, speakers went all over Kentucky encouraging people to support the law. At one level, they seemed to be succeeding. The number of high schools jumped from 54 in 1910 to more than 200 some ten years later. Money per student more than doubled. People felt good about the progress they had made. But the people of Kentucky had a narrow perspective on the matter; they did not see that other states were advancing even faster. By 1940, Kentucky stood last in the nation in the percentage of people who had finished high school, and it took the state a long time to get out of that educational hole.

The second major change occurred when the U.S. Supreme Court invalidated segregation and ruled that black and white students could go to school together.

The third change came in 1990, when the state legislature passed the Kentucky Education Reform Act (KERA). The old approach had not worked very well, and schools in poor counties had an especially hard time. Finally, the state supreme court agreed that the existing educational system did not meet constitutional requirements and ordered that a new one be set up. KERA included several new ways of doing things to make the public schools better.

People knew that the problems had been building for many years and that there would be no quick solutions. Slowly, the changes started to have an effect, however. The differences between Kentucky and the U.S. average became smaller. The state rankings got a little better each year. Not everything that was tried succeeded, so additional changes were made. Still more may be needed in the future. The key change was that people were talking about the schools and what could be done to improve them, rather than just ignoring them.

The question for the future centers on whether state and local backing will continue at a high level. After a good beginning with the 1908 reform and the Whirlwind Campaign, advocacy died down, and education suffered. A strong school system requires continuing support—from students, teachers, parents, leaders, local groups, and state organizations. Everyone has to be a part of it.

Colleges and Universities

After high school, an increasing number of students continue their schooling. Some may attend technical schools to learn special skills or go to two-year community colleges, part of the Kentucky Community and Technical College System. Others may go to colleges that offer four years of higher education or to universities with graduate programs. From the early times, Kentucky has had many colleges and universities.

The first school offering college-level classes was what is now called Transylvania University in Lexington. It started with classes held in a log cabin in Danville in 1785 and later moved to Lexington. For some years, Transylvania was recognized as one of the best schools in the nation. At a time when only ten medical schools existed in the United States, Transylvania had one of them. The college also had a school of law, a fine library, and talented teachers. Before the Civil War, it was the best college in the South, and many famous people studied there. However, problems arose. Religious and political leaders forced one good president to leave, and some of the professors left as well. Its funding decreased, and state support ended. By the time of the Civil War, a weakened Transylvania had closed its school of medicine. It regained some of its strength in the twentieth century, however.

Before the Civil War and for much of the nineteenth century, most people who went to college attended private schools, usually either all-male or all-female ones. That situation did not change until late in the century.

Two other private colleges that were started before the Civil War remain as outstanding schools in Kentucky. Centre College in Danville had Presbyterian Church support, and Georgetown College was the first Baptist college west of the mountains and the fifth one in the nation.

Berea College offered only high school–level classes before the Civil War. It admitted its first college students four years after the conflict ended. Berea differed from other schools at the time because black and white students attended classes together. In 1904, the Day law ordered the school to separate the races. For the next half century, only segregated classes could take place in Kentucky.

During that period, African American schools were established. In Louisville, Simmons University, a private school for blacks, was the first Kentucky college run by African Americans. Later taken over by the

University of Louisville, it became part of that school. Meanwhile, the state also established a public college for African Americans. What is now Kentucky State University in Frankfort opened in 1887 and at first mostly trained people to be teachers.

Other private schools began to open their doors, including more than half a dozen that offered college-level courses to those seeking to become preachers. Some did not last very long; others continue to offer classes today. By the first decade of the twenty-first century, the following private colleges and universities operated in Kentucky: Alice Lloyd College in Pippa Passes, Asbury College in Wilmore, Bellarmine University in Louisville, Berea College, Brescia University in Owensboro, Campbellsville University, Centre College, University of the Cumberlands in Williamsburg, Georgetown College, Kentucky Christian College in Grayson, Kentucky Wesleyan College in Owensboro, Lindsey Wilson College in Columbia, Midway College, Pikeville College, Spalding University in Louisville, Thomas More College in Crestview Hills, Transylvania University, and Union College in Barbourville. More than a half dozen seminaries exist as well. Private colleges remain strong in the state.

Those colleges filled a real need in Kentucky, and they still do. However, they never trained large numbers of students. As higher education grew in importance, a different kind of school was needed. People wanted schools where larger numbers could attend at lower costs. An early leader expressed his dream: "We want a university giving education of the highest order to all classes." He sought a people's college. Out of that need grew what is now the University of Kentucky, the first fully state-supported college. It started in 1865, at the end of the Civil War. About twenty years later, it granted its first degree to a woman. A law school opened early in the twentieth century, and a medical school in the 1960s. The university continued to expand over time.

After the creation of Kentucky State, other state-supported colleges appeared around the commonwealth. In 1906, the state formed what became Eastern Kentucky University in Richmond and Western Kentucky University in Bowling Green. The year 1922 saw the formation of Morehead State University and Murray State University. Northern Kentucky University at Highland Heights came into the system in 1968. The University of Louisville had initially been supported by the city as a kind of municipally funded private college, but in 1970 it too gained

Kentucky Lives: Lyman Johnson

College-educated high school teacher Lyman Johnson and some others were traveling through a small Kentucky town. It was late, and they were hungry, so they went to a restaurant. But when the owner saw that Johnson was African American, he said, "You can't eat in the dining room," and sent him around to the kitchen. Johnson said the food was good; in fact, he said, "They gave us everything but respect." And respect was what Johnson wanted most of all.

Johnson's grandparents had been slaves. He grew up in Tennessee, one of nine children. His father was the principal of a black school. Johnson went to college in Michigan and found himself the only black person in all-white classes. After college he moved to Kentucky and taught for about forty years at Louisville Central High School.

He found that Kentucky resembled Tennessee in many ways. For instance, segregation ruled. If a person went to a dentist, there would be separate chairs for whites and blacks. Black women could go to some stores to buy dresses, but they could not try them on. When Johnson went to the seashore on vacation, he found that African Americans were allowed to use the beach and swim in the ocean only at night. He considered such rules stupid. Johnson once said, "Don't pity me because I live in the slums. Pity yourself that you permit a slum to be."

Johnson decided to change the rules and applied for admission to the University of Kentucky. At that time, all Kentucky schools were segregated. But in 1949, a judge ordered that Johnson should be allowed to attend the university. After that, other colleges opened their classrooms to people of all races. Years later, the University of Kentucky presented Johnson with an honorary doctorate for breaking down those barriers. In Louisville, a school was named for him. Johnson had made a difference. He had earned respect.

state support. Over the years, the state has built a system of higher education that offers students many choices.

College Life

In both public and private colleges in the nineteenth century, the rules were strict for students. Students at the (then) all-male University of Kentucky had this schedule each day:

5:30	Wake-up call
6:00	Room inspection
6:30–7:30	Breakfast
7:30–8:30	Morning study
8:30–9:00	Morning church
9:00–Noon	Classes
Noon–1:00	Lunch
1:00–4:00	Afternoon study
4:00–5:00	Military drill
5:00–6:30	Supper
6:30–9:30	Evening study
10:00	Lights out

College authorities established many rules for the students to follow also. At the University of Kentucky, some 200 regulations included punishment for smoking, playing cards, leaving one's room, not going to church, and many more things. The same kinds of rules existed at private colleges. Before the Civil War, students at Georgetown College could not leave their rooms after seven in the evening. They could not go to barrooms, to places of a noisy and immoral nature, or to the nearby female college. Students were not permitted to participate in duels. Women's colleges had similar rules. As late as the 1920s, one college expelled a young woman for cutting her hair too short.

In the twentieth century, college rules became a little less strict but remained stern until the 1960s. Then, many colleges began to treat stu-

Early dorm room used by students at the University of Kentucky. (Courtesy of the University of Kentucky Special Collections and Archives)

Kentucky Lives: Phillip A. Sharp

In 1993, Phillip A. Sharp was awarded the Nobel Prize (and the sum of $850,000) for his work in medicine. The Kentucky educational system had trained Sharp in his early years.

Sharp grew up near Falmouth in Pendleton County, in the northern part of the state. He wrote in his official Nobel Prize life story: "A sense of place was and remains an important part of my life. . . . My earliest memories are those of a child playing around the house on our family farm, located in a bend of the Licking River. . . . My mother . . . had grown up in that same house."

Sharp attended the public schools of Pendleton County, and his parents always wanted him to go to college. "They taught me to save my money for college tuition," he noted, "and, even more important, they allowed me to earn it by raising cattle for the market and growing tobacco." He went to Union College in eastern Kentucky and majored in math and chemistry. There he met the woman who became his wife and the mother of their three children. Sharp then left Kentucky to pursue his education. He worked under an earlier Nobel Prize winner, headed the Center for Cancer Research, and later worked at the Department of Biology at the Massachusetts Institute of Technology. When Sharp won the Nobel Prize, he was forty-nine years old.

Sharp's Kentucky childhood, with its secure sense of place, had helped form him. The state schools had helped shape his mind. Sharp took it from there and became a leader in his field.

dents like adults and give them more freedom. They could decide when to study (or not to study at all); they could schedule their own classes; they had more freedom to go places and do things. But they had to learn that with such newfound freedom came more responsibility.

By the year 2000, about 17 percent of the people in Kentucky had graduated from college. In the United States overall, about 25 percent are college graduates. The state has been improving, but it still needs to do more. In the future, the level of education may be one of the keys to success both for individuals and for states.

Kentucky schools have helped three people rise to the top of their fields and win the Nobel Prize: Thomas Hunt Morgan of Lexington in 1933; William N. Lipscomb Jr., who grew up in Lexington, in 1976; and Phillip A. Sharp, a native of Falmouth, in 1993.

CHAPTER TWELVE

Today and Tomorrow in Kentucky

One of the reasons people look at the past is to help them understand where they might be going in the future. History can help societies plan for what is to come in the years ahead. But to do that requires knowing about the present—in this case, Kentucky's strengths and weaknesses. That way, people can take the best parts of the past and the present and carry them into the future. They can also cast aside those things that have been detrimental or impeded progress. Studying the past can help identify potential problems in the future and make plans to deal with them.

A Typical Kentuckian

At the start of the twenty-first century, the typical person in Kentucky was a thirty-six-year-old white woman who was likely born in the state. (Kentucky had few foreign immigrants compared with the United States as a whole.) On average, people in Kentucky did not earn as much as the typical American, but the cost of living was less in Kentucky than elsewhere. Kentuckians were more likely to own their homes than the average American, and they made smaller mortgage payments as well. An income gap existed between earnings in Kentucky and earnings in the country overall.

Kentucky in the year 2000 was still a poor state. It ranked forty-fifth of the fifty states in terms of people living in poverty. Almost one in six people in Kentucky lived below the poverty line, compared with one in eight in the whole United States. The state also had a very large gap between rich people and poor people.

In health matters, people in Kentucky tended to be overweight, with high blood pressure. More of them died from heart disease, cancer, and accidents than did people across the nation. The commonwealth also had more people who smoked than any other state. On the positive side, very few people in the state had AIDS, and Kentuckians felt safe in their homes.

In the area of religion, Kentucky was above average in church membership, but it did not rank particularly high. Half of all church members were Baptists; Roman Catholics constituted the second largest denomination. In politics, more people registered Democrat, although many of them voted Republican.

On matters of the environment, Kentucky stood in the middle of the states in air quality. People used a lot of gasoline—the state ranked ninth highest—but overall did well in energy use. In short, at the start of the twenty-first century, there were both good and bad aspects of living in Kentucky.

Saving Parts of the Past

What are some of Kentucky's strengths? What things should citizens try to take into the future?

Kentuckians have a sense of place and a love of their home. That is one thing they may want to take into the future. More than 170 years ago, someone wrote, "Wherever the Kentuckian travels, he earnestly remembers his native hills and plains." A hundred years later, a book told of "the Kentuckian's love of family."

People have pointed to Kentucky writing, music, and folk culture as important things to continue in the future. One person asked, "Are we seriously intent on becoming a region of fast food, or will we eventually learn to cherish and preserve our folk culture?"

Some people stress Kentucky's difference as an asset. In a world where things seem more and more alike, people will be attracted to unique places. The state's horse farms, forests, parks, waterways, friendly people, rich history, and so much more can give it a special place in America's future. As one writer noted, however, "Distinctiveness may easily slip through our fingers."

Saving those things that have made Kentucky different may not be easy. Someone wrote that people must protect past strengths "from what has proved to be the greatest threat to everything in this planet—ourselves." This does not mean that everything old should be preserved just because it is part of the past. Many parts of the past are best forgotten and left behind. Instead, as people go into the future, they should remember what has made Kentucky special. How the future unfolds is partly in the hands of people living now. They must use that power well.

Identifying Future Issues

A baseball player once said, "Predictions are hard, especially about the future." Trying to identify the important issues of the future is difficult because conditions change. Something that seems likely to be a problem in the future might suddenly be resolved because of a new invention or some other change. But at the same time, people cannot just wait for the future to happen; they have to plan for it, no matter how uncertain that planning might be. Most of all, individuals have to get their minds ready for the future. As one person wrote, "We must learn to embrace change and become more flexible and less afraid of the new." Yet Kentuckians must not be afraid of keeping the best parts of the old. Finding the right balance may be the hardest part.

At the beginning of the twenty-first century, a number of people were

---

Kentucky Lives: John Uri Lloyd

One of the first science fiction novels written in America was by a Kentuckian. John Uri Lloyd came to the state at age four and grew up in Boone and Grant counties in northern Kentucky. Later he wrote a series of novels about that area, the most famous being *Stringtown on the Pike* (1900).

Lloyd went to work at age fourteen in a drugstore and later became a famous druggist himself. He wrote many books about how to use plants and other natural approaches to healing. With the money he made from those books, he built a large library that still exists in Cincinnati. Lloyd's wife died only eleven days after they were married, and he went back to work to try to forget his grief.

His first novel, *Etidorhpa,* appeared in 1895. It was very unusual, because almost no one wrote science fiction at the time. It tells of a man's journey to the center of the earth via some deep caves near Smithland, Kentucky. Lloyd presented the story as if someone else had written it and had given it to him to transform into a book. In the novel, an eyeless, faceless, blue-skinned guide leads the hero downward, where he finds a strange underground world of giant mushrooms, huge lakes, odd animals, and new rules of motion. At the earth's center, he also finds the mother of love—Etidorhpa. Although the book would not be considered great writing by today's standards, it was one of the first attempts to make people think about the future and things unknown.

asked what they considered the most important issues facing Kentucky in the future. Some people pointed to the use of the land. Will the future pollute it or protect it? Others noted the rapid growth of technology, such as computers. Technology can move a state forward into new areas, but as a high school student stated, "We must control technology and not let it control us, or we will destroy ourselves."

Some suggested that in the future, people in Kentucky must be better prepared to be a part of a "new economy." The old ways of earning a living will change, and education will be the key to adjusting to that change. In the future it will be more important to continue learning after school and to keep up with innovations in technology, information, and the global marketplace. States with an educated citizenry that can adapt to a changing economy will prosper.

Other people stressed issues that have been around for a long time. For example, some believe that Kentuckians must work harder to treat all people as equals, end hunger and poverty, and resolve conflicts peacefully. Some of those questioned about the future emphasized the need to find new power sources, such as solar or hydrogen power. Others stressed better health care for longer lives. But all those questioned agreed with one study of the future that said, "Change has been the one constant in our lives."

The Future

What will the future bring? A few years ago, one group asked people in Kentucky what needed to be done to make things better in the future. They came up with twenty-six goals. The question remains: can the citizens of Kentucky make them a reality?

Some people may complain about how bad things are now. They may say that one person alone cannot do anything to change things. But that is not the right perspective for our times. As one person said: "Our ancestors faced worse. And I think no matter what trials we face, somebody born today always has a chance to effect some positive change, to find their place in the world and do something good."

One person *can* make a difference—just think of the young boy who saved Abraham Lincoln from drowning in a Kentucky creek, or the handicapped Madge Breckinridge working for women's rights. The way to make the future better is simply to work at making it better. A student

Kentucky Voices

In 1992—200 years after statehood—Kentucky created the Long-Term Policy Research Center to provide people with information and perspective so that they could make better decisions in the future. After receiving comments from numerous people, the center came up with twenty-six goals for the future:

Goal 1: Kentucky communities will be safe and caring places that enable all citizens to lead productive, fulfilling lives.

Goal 2: Kentucky's communities and citizens will share responsibility in helping families succeed.

Goal 3: Kentuckians will have decent, safe, and affordable housing.

Goal 4: All Kentuckians will have access to affordable, high-quality, and comprehensive health care.

Goal 5: Kentucky communities will have high levels of trust and civic pride, realized from broad citizen participation.

Goal 6: Kentucky communities will value and respect all individuals, regardless of culture, race, ethnic background, religion, or gender.

Goal 7: Kentuckians will have an educational system of lifelong learning.

Goal 8: Kentuckians will have equal opportunity to obtain an internationally competitive education.

Goal 9: Kentucky's children will come to school ready and able to learn.

Goal 10: Kentucky children will have safe, stable learning environments.

Goal 11: Kentuckians will promote partnerships among parents, schools, and communities to enhance the social and academic development of children.

Goal 12: Kentuckians will have opportunities to appreciate, participate in, and contribute to the arts and humanities.

Goal 13: Kentucky will end poverty.

Goal 14: Kentucky will have diversified long-term development that stresses competitiveness and a rising standard of living for all citizens.

Goal 15: Kentucky will benefit from participation in an integrated global economy.

Goal 16: Kentucky will maintain and enhance a strong farm economy.

Goal 17: Kentucky will develop and enhance its physical infrastructure to support and sustain economic development and a high quality of life.

Goal 18: Kentucky will develop a state-of-the-art technological infrastructure that complements its learning culture and bolsters its competitive position in the world economy. ▶

Goal 19: Kentucky will establish a fair . . . tax structure.

Goal 20: Kentucky will create an entrepreneurial economy.

Goal 21: Kentucky will protect and enhance its environment.

Goal 22: Individuals, communities, and businesses will use resources wisely and reduce waste through recycling.

Goal 23: Kentucky communities will foster and promote a high level of environmental awareness and pollution abatement.

Goal 24: Government at all levels will be . . . responsive to the changing needs of Kentuckians.

Goal 25: Kentucky will ensure a fair, equitable, and effective system of justice.

Goal 26: Citizens should continue to broaden their understanding of issues, play a role in the civic life of their communities, and recognize the enduring importance of their participation.

near Louisville said in the year 2000: "We should be a nation of doers. We should be out there and we should be doing stuff." A high school student in Nelson County said it very clearly: "If we want these things to change, that's the only way it's going to happen—if we do it ourselves."

For year after year, century after century, people have faced problems and issues. Some were the same problems we face today; some were different. Some were solved; some were not. But they tried. We now have more tools available to help us deal with our problems than ever before. We just need to work and try. The future awaits us all.

Kentucky Counties

County	County Seat	Year Created	2000 Population	Origin of County Name
Adair	Columbia	1801	17,244	Governor John Adair
Allen	Scottsville	1815	17,800	John Allen, killed in Indian wars
Anderson	Lawrenceburg	1827	19,111	Richard C. Anderson Jr., public official
Ballard	Wickliffe	1842	8,286	Bland W. Ballard, Indian fighter
Barren	Glasgow	1798	38,033	The Barrens, name of a section of the state
Bath	Owingsville	1811	11,085	Healthy springs there
Bell	Pineville	1867	30,060	Joshua F. Bell, political leader
Boone	Burlington	1798	85,991	Daniel Boone
Bourbon	Paris	1785	19,360	Royal family of France
Boyd	Catlettsburg	1860	49,752	Linn Boyd, Speaker of U.S. House of Representatives from Kentucky
Boyle	Danville	1842	27,697	Chief Justice John Boyle
Bracken	Brooksville	1796	8,279	William Bracken, area pioneer
Breathitt	Jackson	1839	16,100	Governor John Breathitt
Breckinridge	Hardinsburg	1799	18,648	U.S. Attorney General John Breckinridge of Kentucky
Bullitt	Shepherdsville	1796	61,236	Lt. Governor Alexander S. Bullitt
Butler	Morgantown	1810	13,010	General Richard Butler, killed in Indian wars
Caldwell	Princeton	1809	13,060	Lt. Governor John Caldwell
Calloway	Murray	1822	34,177	Pioneer Richard Calloway
Campbell	Alexandria and Newport	1794	88,616	Pioneer John Campbell

*The spelling of the county name is different from the spelling of the person's name.

County	County Seat	Year Created	2000 Population	Origin of County Name
Carlisle	Bardwell	1886	5,351	U.S. Secretary of the Treasury John G. Carlisle of Kentucky
Carroll	Carrollton	1838	10,155	Charles Carroll, signer of Declaration of Independence
Carter	Grayson	1838	26,889	William G. Carter, state senator
Casey	Liberty	1806	15,447	Pioneer William Casey
Christian	Hopkinsville	1796	72,265	William Christian, killed in Indian wars
Clark	Winchester	1792	33,144	General George Rogers Clark
Clay	Manchester	1806	24,556	Pioneer Green Clay
Clinton	Albany	1835	9,634	New York Governor DeWitt Clinton
Crittenden	Marion	1842	9,384	Governor John J. Crittenden
Cumberland	Burkesville	1798	7,147	Cumberland River
Daviess	Owensboro	1815	91,545	Joseph H. Daveiss,* killed in Indian wars
Edmonson	Brownsville	1825	11,644	John Edmonson, killed in Indian wars
Elliott	Sandy Hook	1869	6,748	Judge John M. Elliott
Estill	Irvine	1808	15,307	James Estill, killed in Indian wars
Fayette	Lexington	1780	260,512	General Lafayette of France
Fleming	Flemingsburg	1798	13,792	Pioneer John Fleming
Floyd	Prestonsburg	1799	42,441	Pioneer John Floyd
Franklin	Frankfort	1794	47,687	Benjamin Franklin
Fulton	Hickman	1845	7,752	Steamboat inventor Robert Fulton
Gallatin	Warsaw	1798	7,870	U.S. Secretary of the Treasury Albert Gallatin
Garrard	Lancaster	1796	14,792	Governor James Garrard
Grant	Williamstown	1820	22,384	Samuel Grant, killed by Indians
Graves	Mayfield	1823	37,028	Benjamin Graves, killed in Indian wars

County	County Seat	Year Created	2000 Population	Origin of County Name
Grayson	Leitchfield	1810	24,053	William Grayson, Virginia senator
Green	Greensburg	1792	11,518	General Nathanael Greene* of Rhode Island
Greenup	Greenup	1803	36,891	Governor Christopher Greenup
Hancock	Hawesville	1829	8,392	John Hancock, signer of Declaration of Independence
Hardin	Elizabethtown	1792	94,174	John Hardin, killed in Indian wars
Harlan	Harlan	1819	33,202	Silas Harlan, killed in Indian wars
Harrison	Cynthiana	1793	17,983	Benjamin Harrison, legislator
Hart	Munfordville	1819	17,445	N. G. T. Hart, killed in Indian wars
Henderson	Henderson	1798	44,829	Richard Henderson, landowner
Henry	New Castle	1798	15,060	Virginia Governor Patrick Henry
Hickman	Clinton	1821	5,262	Paschal Hickman, killed in Indian wars
Hopkins	Madisonville	1806	46,519	General Samuel Hopkins
Jackson	McKee	1858	13,495	President Andrew Jackson
Jefferson	Louisville	1780	693,604	President Thomas Jefferson
Jessamine	Nicholasville	1798	39,041	Settler Jessamine Douglas
Johnson	Paintsville	1843	23,445	Vice President Richard M. Johnson of Kentucky
Kenton	Independence and Covington	1840	151,464	Pioneer Simon Kenton
Knott	Hindman	1884	17,649	Governor J. Proctor Knott
Knox	Barbourville	1799	31,795	Revolutionary War General Henry Knox
Larue	Hodgenville	1843	13,373	Pioneer John Larue
Laurel	London	1825	52,715	Laurel River
Lawrence	Louisa	1821	15,569	Naval officer James Lawrence
Lee	Beattyville	1870	7,916	Probably General Robert E. Lee of Virginia

County	County Seat	Year Created	2000 Population	Origin of County Name
Leslie	Hyden	1878	12,401	Governor Preston Leslie
Letcher	Whitesburg	1842	25,277	Governor Robert Letcher
Lewis	Vanceburg	1806	14,092	Meriwether Lewis of Lewis and Clark expedition
Lincoln	Stanford	1780	23,361	General Benjamin Lincoln of Virginia
Livingston	Smithland	1798	9,804	Robert Livingston of N.Y., signer of Declaration of Independence
Logan	Russellville	1792	26,573	Pioneer Benjamin Logan
Lyon	Eddyville	1854	8,080	Congressman Matthew Lyon
Madison	Richmond	1785	70,872	President James Madison
Magoffin	Salyersville	1860	13,332	Governor Beriah Magoffin
Marion	Lebanon	1834	18,212	General Francis Marion of South Carolina
Marshall	Benton	1842	30,125	U.S. Supreme Court Chief Justice John Marshall
Martin	Inez	1870	12,578	Congressman John P. Martin
Mason	Maysville	1788	16,800	Virginia legislator George Mason
McCracken	Paducah	1824	65,514	Virgil McCracken, killed in Indian wars
McCreary	Whitley City	1912	17,080	Governor James McCreary
McLean	Calhoun	1854	9,938	Judge Alney McLean
Meade	Brandenburg	1823	26,349	James Meade, killed in Indian wars
Menifee	Frenchburg	1869	6,556	Congressman Richard Menefee*
Mercer	Harrodsburg	1785	20, 817	General Hugh Mercer of Virginia
Metcalfe	Edmonton	1860	10,037	Governor Thomas Metcalfe
Monroe	Tompkinsville	1820	11,756	President James Monroe
Montgomery	Mt. Sterling	1796	22,554	General Richard Montgomery, killed in Revolutionary War
Morgan	West Liberty	1822	13,948	General Daniel Morgan of Virginia

County	County Seat	Year Created	2000 Population	Origin of County Name
Muhlenberg	Greenville	1798	31,839	Revolutionary War General Peter Muhlenberg
Nelson	Bardstown	1784	37,477	Revolutionary War General Thomas Nelson of Virginia
Nicholas	Carlisle	1799	6,813	Lawyer George Nicholas
Ohio	Hartford	1798	22,916	Ohio River
Oldham	LaGrange	1823	46,178	William Oldham, killed in Indian wars
Owen	Owenton	1819	10,547	Abraham Owen, killed in Indian wars
Owsley	Booneville	1843	4,858	Governor William Owsley
Pendleton	Falmouth	1798	14,390	Congressman Edmund Pendleton of Virginia
Perry	Hazard	1820	29,390	Navy hero Oliver Hazard Perry
Pike	Pikeville	1821	68,736	Explorer Zebulon Pike
Powell	Stanton	1852	13,237	Governor Lazarus Powell
Pulaski	Somerset	1798	56,217	Revolutionary War General Joseph Pulaski of Poland
Robertson	Mt. Olivet	1867	2,266	Kentucky Judge George Robertson
Rockcastle	Mt. Vernon	1810	16,582	Rockcastle River
Rowan	Morehead	1856	22,094	Kentucky Judge John Rowan
Russell	Jamestown	1825	16,315	Colonel William Russell
Scott	Georgetown	1792	33,061	Governor Charles Scott
Shelby	Shelbyville	1792	33,337	Governor Isaac Shelby
Simpson	Franklin	1819	16,405	John Simpson, killed in Indian wars
Spencer	Taylorsville	1824	11,766	Spears Spencer, killed in Indian wars
Taylor	Campbellsville	1848	22,927	President Zachary Taylor
Todd	Elkton	1819	11,971	John Todd, killed in Indian wars
Trigg	Cadiz	1820	12,597	Stephen Trigg, killed in Indian wars

County	County Seat	Year Created	2000 Population	Origin of County Name
Trimble	Bedford	1836	8,125	U.S. Supreme Court Judge Robert Trimble of Kentucky
Union	Morganfield	1811	15,637	Uncertain
Warren	Bowling Green	1796	92,522	Revolutionary War General Joseph Warren
Washington	Springfield	1792	10,916	President George Washington
Wayne	Monticello	1800	19,923	General "Mad Anthony" Wayne
Webster	Dixon	1860	14,120	Senator Daniel Webster of Massachusetts
Whitley	Williamsburg	1818	35,865	Pioneer William Whitley
Wolfe	Campton	1860	7,065	Louisville lawyer Nathaniel Wolfe
Woodford	Versailles	1788	23,208	General William Woodford of Virginia

Kentucky's Governors

Isaac Shelby (1792–1796 and 1812–1816): of Lincoln County; native of Maryland; surveyor and soldier; active in the American Revolution and frontier campaigns against the Indians; counties in nine states are named in his honor.

James Garrard (1796–1804): of Bourbon County; born in Virginia; Revolutionary War soldier; first to live in the governor's mansion (today the residence of the lieutenant governor); only Kentucky governor to serve two full successive terms until Paul Patton (1995–2003).

Christopher Greenup (1804–1808): of Mercer and Fayette counties; born in Virginia; soldier; one of the first two Kentucky representatives in Congress after Kentucky entered the Union; elected governor without opposition.

Charles Scott (1808–1812): of Woodford County; born in Virginia; soldier; officer in the Braddock expedition (1755); represented Woodford County in the Virginia Assembly.

George Madison (1816): of Franklin County; born in Virginia; Revolutionary War soldier; Indian fighter; hero in War of 1812—captured at River Raisin; died in office.

Gabriel Slaughter (1816–1820): of Mercer County; born in Virginia; farmer; regimental commander at Battle of New Orleans; twice lieutenant governor; became governor upon Madison's death.

John Adair (1820–1824): of Mercer County; born in South Carolina; Revolutionary War soldier; fought in Indian wars; aide to Governor Isaac Shelby in Battle of the Thames (1813); elected to U.S. House of Representatives for one term (1831–1833).

Joseph Desha (1824–1828): of Mason County; born in Pennsylvania; soldier in Indian campaigns; commander in Battle of the Thames (1813); state legislator; served in U.S. House of Representatives (1807–1819).

Thomas Metcalfe (1828–1832): of Nicholas County; born in Virginia; stonemason—nicknamed "Old Stonehammer"; soldier in the War of 1812; served ten years as U.S. congressman and senator; died during cholera epidemic of 1855.

Adapted from James C. Klotter, ed., *Our Kentucky: A Study of the Bluegrass State* (Lexington: University Press of Kentucky, 2000).

John Breathitt (1832–1834): of Logan County; born in Virginia; lawyer; previously served in Kentucky legislature and as lieutenant governor; died in office.

James Turner Morehead (1834–1836): of Logan County; lieutenant governor who became governor upon Breathitt's death; U.S. senator (1841–1847); political ally of Henry Clay, a fellow Whig.

James Clark (1836–1839): of Clark County; born in Virginia; served in Kentucky legislature; as judge, rendered the decision that started the Old and New Court fight; died in office.

Charles Anderson Wickliffe (1839–1840): of Nelson County; lawyer; six-term U.S. congressman; became governor upon Clark's death; postmaster general for President John Tyler (1841–1845); grandfather of Governor J. C. W. Beckham.

Robert P. Letcher (1840–1844): of Mercer (later Garrard) County; born in Virginia; Whig; lawyer; served in state legislature and U.S. Congress; American minister (ambassador) to Mexico (1849–1852).

William Owsley (1844–1848): of Lincoln County; born in Virginia; Whig; lawyer; served in state legislature; longtime justice of Kentucky Court of Appeals.

John Jordan Crittenden (1848–1850): of Woodford County; Whig; lawyer; saw service in War of 1812 as aide to Shelby and was present at Battle of the Thames; resigned governorship to become U.S. attorney general; served total of twenty years in U.S. Senate.

John L. Helm (1850–1851 and 1867): of Hardin County; succeeded Crittenden in 1850; elected in his own right sixteen years later but died in office; state legislator; openly sympathetic to the Confederate cause.

Lazarus W. Powell (1851–1855): of Henderson County; Democratic lawyer; state legislator; U.S. senator; favored Kentucky neutrality during the Civil War.

Charles Slaughter Morehead (1855–1859): of Nelson County; lawyer; two-term Whig member of Congress; elected governor on American (Know-Nothing) Party ticket.

Beriah Magoffin (1859–1862): of Mercer County; Democrat; lawyer; resigned because of his Confederate sympathies but was permitted to name his successor.

James F. Robinson (1862–1863): of Scott County; lawyer; Whig state senator, staunch Unionist Democrat.

Thomas E. Bramlette (1863–1867): of Cumberland (now Clinton) County; lawyer and circuit judge; commissioned in Union army.

John W. Stevenson (1867–1871): of Kenton County; born in Virginia; Democrat; lieutenant governor who assumed office upon Helm's death; U.S. senator (1871–1877).

Preston H. Leslie (1871–1875): of Clinton County; Democrat; lawyer and state legislator; accepted appointment in 1887 as governor of Montana Territory, where he died in 1907.

James Bennett McCreary (1875–1879 and 1911–1915): of Madison County; Democrat; lawyer; Confederate soldier with Generals Morgan and Breckinridge; served eighteen years in U.S. House and Senate; first to occupy the new governor's mansion (1914).

Dr. Luke P. Blackburn (1879–1883): of Woodford County; Democrat; first physician to serve as Kentucky governor; volunteer during cholera and yellow fever epidemics in Kentucky and throughout the South; prison reformer.

J. Proctor Knott (1883–1887): of Marion County; Democrat; lawyer, congressman, and noted orator; attorney general of Missouri before returning to Kentucky in 1862; one of the framers of the present Kentucky Constitution.

Simon Bolivar Buckner (1887–1891): of Hart County; Democrat; West Point instructor; served in the Mexican War and later with the Confederacy; editor of the *Louisville Courier*.

John Young Brown (1891–1895): of Hardin County; Democrat; lawyer; congressman; his "three-year legislature" adjusted laws to the new constitution.

William O. Bradley (1895–1899): of Garrard County; lawyer; first Republican governor; U.S. senator (1909–1914).

William S. Taylor (1899–1900): of Butler County; lawyer; Republican; Kentucky attorney general; lost the governorship to William Goebel in a contest decided by the legislature.

William Goebel (1900): of Kenton County; born in Pennsylvania; Democrat; lawyer; state senator; declared governor after being shot on the grounds of the Old Capitol; only governor in U.S. history to die in office as a result of assassination.

John Crepps Wickliffe Beckham (1900–1907): of Nelson County; Democrat; lawyer and state legislator; speaker of Kentucky House; elected lieutenant governor on Goebel ticket and succeeded to governorship upon his death; U.S. senator (1915–1921); grandson of Governor Charles Anderson Wickliffe.

Augustus E. Willson (1907–1911): of Jefferson County; born in Mason County; law partner of John Marshall Harlan; five-time unsuccessful Republican nominee for U.S. House or Senate.

Augustus Owsley Stanley (1915–1919): of Henderson County; born in Shelby County; Democrat; lawyer; served six terms in U.S. House; elected to U.S. Senate in 1918; resigned as governor in 1919; later chaired International Joint Commission to mediate disputes arising along the U.S.-Canadian border.

James D. Black (1919): of Knox County; Democrat; lawyer; state legislator; assistant attorney general of Kentucky; as lieutenant governor, succeeded Stanley; defeated for election in his own right.

Edwin Porch Morrow (1919–1923): of Pulaski County; Republican lawyer; soldier in Spanish-American War; U.S. district attorney; nephew of Governor William O. Bradley.

William J. Fields (1923–1927): of Carter County; Democrat; resigned after almost thirteen years in Congress to become governor; called "Honest Bill of Olive Hill."

Flem D. Sampson (1927–1931): of Knox County; born in Laurel County; Republican lawyer; circuit judge; chief justice of Kentucky Court of Appeals.

Ruby Laffoon (1931–1935): of Hopkins County; Democrat; lawyer; chairman of first Insurance Rating Board in Kentucky; Hopkins County judge.

Albert Benjamin Chandler (1935–1939 and 1955–1959): of Woodford County; born in Henderson County; Democrat; lawyer; state senator; lieutenant governor; resigned in 1939 to become U.S. senator; commissioner of baseball; nicknamed "Happy."

Keen Johnson (1939–1943): of Madison County; born in Lyon County; Democrat; publisher of *Richmond Daily Register;* lieutenant governor who assumed office upon Chandler's resignation; elected in his own right that same year.

Simeon Willis (1943–1947): of Boyd County; born in Ohio; lawyer; appointed to state court of appeals; member of Republican National Committee.

Earle C. Clements (1947–1950): of Union County; Democrat; served in U.S. Army during World War I; sheriff; county clerk; county judge; state senator; congressman; resigned governorship in 1950 to assume seat in U.S. Senate.

Lawrence W. Wetherby (1950–1955): of Jefferson County; Democrat; lawyer; judge of Jefferson County Juvenile Court; lieutenant governor who became governor upon Clements's resignation; elected to office in his own right in 1951.

Bert T. Combs (1959–1963): of Floyd County; born in Clay County; Democrat; served in World War II; lawyer; Kentucky Court of Appeals judge (1951–1955); judge on U.S. Court of Appeals, Sixth Circuit (1967–1970).

Edward (Ned) T. Breathitt Jr. (1963–1967): of Christian County; lawyer; served in state legislature (1952–1958); later a railroad executive.

Louie B. Nunn (1967–1971): of Barren County; Republican; lawyer; elected county judge of Barren County; city attorney of Glasgow.

Wendell H. Ford (1971–1974): of Daviess County; Democrat; state senator; lieutenant governor; resigned governorship to assume seat in U.S. Senate.

Julian M. Carroll (1974–1979): of McCracken County; Democrat; member of Kentucky House of Representatives (1962–1971); speaker of Kentucky house; lieutenant governor who became governor upon Ford's resignation; elected to office in his own right in 1975.

John Young Brown Jr. (1979–1983): of Fayette County; attorney; successful business executive (Kentucky Fried Chicken); involved in the ownership of professional sports teams.

Martha Layne Collins (1983–1987): of Shelby and Woodford counties; schoolteacher and home economist; Democrat; elected clerk of Kentucky Court of Appeals in 1975 and lieutenant governor four years later; first woman to be elected governor of Kentucky.

Wallace Wilkinson (1987–1991): of Casey and Fayette counties; Democrat; prominent businessman and real estate developer; instrumental in the revitalization of downtown Lexington.

Brereton Jones (1991–1995): of Woodford County; born in Ohio; Democrat; West Virginia legislator; Kentucky horse farm owner; lieutenant governor.

Paul Patton (1995–2003): of Pike County; born in Lawrence County; Democrat; engineer and businessman; lieutenant governor.

Ernest L. Fletcher (2003–2007): of Fayette County; born in Montgomery County; medical doctor; Republican member of Kentucky House of Representatives; U.S. congressman.

Steven L. Beshear (2007–): of Hopkins County; Democrat; state attorney general; lieutenant governor.

Kentuckians on the U.S. Supreme Court

Thomas Todd of Danville and Frankfort
Robert Trimble of Paris
John McKinley* of Frankfort and Louisville
Samuel Miller* of Richmond and Barbourville
John Marshall Harlan of Danville, Harrodsburg, and Frankfort
Horace Lurton* of Newport
James McReynolds of Elkton
Louis Brandeis* of Louisville
Stanley Reed of Maysville
Wiley Rutledge* of Cloverport
Fred Vinson of Louisa

* Either born in Kentucky or lived there for a period of time, but named to the Court while living in another state.

Kentucky Facts

Area: 40,395 square miles
Population: 4,041,769 (in 2000)
Capital: Frankfort
Counties: 120
U.S. representatives: 6
U.S. senators: 2
State representatives: 100
State senators: 38
State song: "My Old Kentucky Home"
Nickname: Bluegrass State
Statehood: June 1, 1792 (fifteenth state)
State motto: "United we stand; divided we fall"
State musical instrument: Appalachian dulcimer
State bird: Kentucky cardinal
State horse: Thoroughbred
State flower: Goldenrod
State tree: Tulip poplar
State animal: Gray squirrel
State fish: Kentucky bass
State insect: Viceroy butterfly
State fossil: Brachiopod
State mineral: Coal
State gemstone: Freshwater pearl

Additional Sources for Research

These books contain a wealth of information about Kentucky:

Harrison, Lowell H., and James C. Klotter. *A New History of Kentucky*. Lexington: University Press of Kentucky, 1997.

Kleber, John, ed. *The Kentucky Encyclopedia*. Lexington: University Press of Kentucky, 1992.

Ulack, Richard, and Karl Raitz, eds. *Atlas of Kentucky*. Lexington: University Press of Kentucky, 1998.

Other general books include the following:

Irvin, Helen. *Women in Kentucky*. Lexington: University Press of Kentucky, 1979.

Kleber, John, ed. *The Encyclopedia of Louisville*. Lexington: University Press of Kentucky, 2001.

Klotter, James C., ed. *Our Kentucky: A Study of the Bluegrass State*. 2nd ed. Lexington: University Press of Kentucky, 2000.

Lewis, R. Barry, ed. *Kentucky Archaeology*. Lexington: University Press of Kentucky, 1996.

Lucas, Marion B., and George C. Wright. *A History of Blacks in Kentucky*. 2 vols. Frankfort: Kentucky Historical Society, 1992.

Rennick, Robert M. *Kentucky Place Names*. Lexington: University Press of Kentucky, 1984.

Ward, William S. *A Literary History of Kentucky*. Knoxville: University of Tennessee Press, 1988.

For more in-depth study of different time periods, see the following:

Friend, Craig, ed. *The Buzzel about Kentuck: Settling the Promised Land*. Lexington: University Press of Kentucky, 1999.

Harrison, Lowell H. *The Civil War in Kentucky*. 2nd ed. Lexington: University Press of Kentucky, 1987.

Klotter, James C. *Kentucky: Portrait in Paradox, 1900–1950*. Frankfort: Kentucky Historical Society, 1996.

Tapp, Hambleton, and James C. Klotter. *Kentucky: Decades of Discord, 1865–1900.* Frankfort: Kentucky Historical Society, 1977.

These two historical journals have many good articles on Kentucky:

Ohio Valley History (formerly the *Filson Historical Quarterly,* which started in 1926), with a brief listing of articles in a 1987 issue and online.

The Register of the Kentucky Historical Society (printed from 1903 on), with a general index in a 1989 issue.

Among the many online sources, see the Kentucky Virtual Library, with its Digital Library, at www.kyvl.org.

Index

Italic page numbers refer to illustrations